Cacti 0.8 Network Monitoring

Monitor your network with ease!

Dinangkur Kundu

S. M. Ibrahim Lavlu

BIRMINGHAM - MUMBAI

Cacti 0.8 Network Monitoring

First published: August 2009

Production Reference: 1280709

Published by Packt Publishing Ltd.
32 Lincoln Road
Olton
Birmingham, B27 6PA, UK.

ISBN 978-1-847195-96-8

www.packtpub.com

Cover Image by Vinayak Chittar (vinayak.chittar@gmail.com)

Credits

Authors

Dinangkur Kundu

S. M. Ibrahim Lavlu

Reviewers

Andrei-Silviu Marinache

J.P. Pasnak, CD

Acquisition Editor

Rashmi Phadnis

Technical Editor

Ajay Shanker

Indexer

Hemangini Bari

Editorial Team Leader

Abhijeet Deobhakta

Project Team Leader

Lata Basantani

Project Coordinator

Neelkanth Mehta

Proofreaders

Claire Lane

Sandra Hopper

Production Coordinator

Aparna Bhagat

Cover Work

Aparna Bhagat

About the Authors

Dinangkur Kundu is currently working as an IT Support Analyst at Moriah College in Sydney, Australia. He also runs a local business directory for Bangladeshi people and in his free time, develops web sites using concrete5 CMS.

Dinangkur started his career as a Visual Basic programmer for DEN—a hospital management system development company. Later, he moved to Web programming and spent the majority of his career in the Web arena, using open source technologies that are the driving point of his technological advances. He worked as a LAMP developer for Quantumcloud—building and implementing e-commerce solutions, content management systems, helpdesk, and service oriented applications; as Chief Technical Officer, he implemented and managed Linux-based Internet gateways, mail, backup, revision control, and over all security. On rare occasions, he's away from his computer and you can find him reading books on String theory and gazing at Math books.

I dedicate this book—Dipty Rani Kundu and Ranjit Kumar Kundu, most extraordinary and beloved ones in my life, because of your love and blessing I am here and continuing my journey.

I also thank my sweet wife Suravi Sarkar for her faithful support in writing this book. Specially, my younger brother Shanku, who took care of Mum and Dad in my absence, and pushed me to reach my goal.

I want to thank Rashmi Phandis at Packt Publishing for being so patient with me.

S. M. Ibrahim Lavlu is a Linux wizard who has dedicated most of his time to Linux and open source. All the time he is busy with his technical world. He is also an expert in PHP. He is currently working as a software engineer and deployment engineer at Net Ltd. He maintains the world's largest Bangla blog community (www.somewhereinblog.net) and also the busiest site of Bangladesh. In his free time, Lavlu shares his knowledge on www.lavluda.com about his many tutorials and technical documents.

For successfully completing this book, all credit goes to my wife Tania Sabnam (www.tsabnam.com). And special thanks to the Cacti developer team for their great support.

About the Reviewers

Andrei-Silviu Marinache is 29 years old, and he has been working with computers since he was 8 years old. He began to like Linux and networks in the 9th grade, at high school. He often skipped classes just to spend a little more time on the Internet, in the high school's informatics laboratory. He has now more than 12 years of network-experience, a Master's in Informatics Security and works as a System Engineer for one of the biggest telecommunication companies in Romania.

Andrei began to use Cacti when version 0.8 appeared, and since then he continuously tweaked, bug-fixed, and improved it to suit his needs. Some of his patches were made available to the Cacti forum and to the Cacti team.

> I'd like to thank to my wife, because she loves me, even though she can't understand why I sometimes go to sleep at 4 AM, to my mom because she supported me in my career, and to my dad, who built my first computer, a ZX-Spectrum clone.

J.P. Pasnak, CD is a Technical Analyst working on Operational Support Systems for a Canadian Telecommunications Company, a Senior Non-Commissioned Officer in the Canadian Forces Reserves, an avid supporter of Open Source projects, and a member of the Cacti Group.

Table of Contents

Preface

Cacti is a web-based, PHP/MySQL graphing solution to monitor network bandwidth with SNMP using the RRDTool engine—developed by Tobi Oeticker who is already the creator of the famous MRTG. RRDtool is a program developed in C and it stores collected data on `.rrd` files. Cacti's strength lies in the fact that it can be installed and used easily. You don't need to be a guru or spend hours to configure it. Also, the official forum for Cacti is very active and supports Cacti users and there are lots of Cacti templates that can save your time. You can also add plug-ins to Cacti enabling the possibility of integration with other open source tools such as ntop or PHP Weathermap. This is the best RRDtool frontend.

What this book covers

Chapter 1 is an overview of Cacti.

Chapter 2 covers the installation of Cacti on a Linux machine using both APT and a manual installation.

Chapter 3 covers creating devices, adding graph templates, and monitoring network-attached devices.

Chapter 4 covers the creation and usage of templates in Cacti.

Chapter 5 covers the creation of users in Cacti and assigning permissions to view and edit graphs, also assigning realm permissions to access the management console to manage devices.

Chapter 6 covers how Simple Network Management Protocol works—its process to work with network-attached SNMP-enabled devices. We'll also see how Net-SNMP application suite implements SNMP and Cacti uses Net-SNMP to retrieve raw data from managed-system, and then uses the RRDTool to create graphs for easy understanding.

Chapter 7 covers the creation of a new data input method and data query. Also, we'll learn the details of SNMP query XML and Script query XML. At the end of this chapter, we'll see how to create a graph for a single SNMP OID.

Chapter 8 will cover some advanced topics like: Cacti's directory structure, Cacti's backup procedure, Cacti's restore procedure, and Cacti's CLI features.

Who this book is for

This book is for anyone who wants to manage a network using Cacti. You don't have to be a Linux Guru to use this book.

Conventions

In this book, you will find a number of styles of text that distinguish between different kinds of information. Here are some examples of these styles, and an explanation of their meaning.

Code words in text are shown as follows: "We can include other contexts through the use of the include directive."

A block of code will be set as follows:

```
$database_type = "mysql";
$database_default = "cacti";
$database_hostname = "localhost";
$database_username = "cactiuser";
```

Any command-line input or output is written as follows:

```
$ apt-get install php5 libapache2-mod-php5
$/etc/init.d/apache2 restart
```

New terms and **important words** are shown in bold. Words that you see on the screen, in menus or dialog boxes for example, appear in our text like this: "clicking the **Next** button moves you to the next screen".

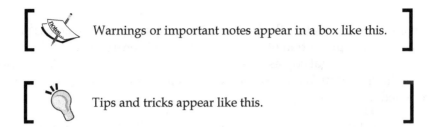

Warnings or important notes appear in a box like this.

Tips and tricks appear like this.

Reader feedback

Feedback from our readers is always welcome. Let us know what you think about this book—what you liked or may have disliked. Reader feedback is important for us to develop titles that you really get the most out of.

To send us general feedback, simply drop an email to feedback@packtpub.com, and mention the book title in the subject of your message.

If there is a book that you need and would like to see us publish, please send us a note via the **SUGGEST A TITLE** form on www.packtpub.com, or send an email to suggest@packtpub.com.

If there is a topic that you have expertise in and you are interested in either writing or contributing to a book on, see our author guide on www.packtpub.com/authors.

Customer support

Now that you are the proud owner of a Packt book, we have a number of things to help you to get the most from your purchase.

Errata

Although we have taken every care to ensure the accuracy of our contents, mistakes do happen. If you find a mistake in one of our books—maybe a mistake in text or code—we would be grateful if you would report this to us. By doing so, you can save other readers from frustration, and help us to improve subsequent versions of this book. If you find any errata, please report them by visiting http://www.packtpub.com/support, selecting your book, clicking on the **let us know** link, and entering the details of your errata. Once your errata are verified, your submission will be accepted and the errata added to any list of existing errata. Any existing errata can be viewed by selecting your title from http://www.packtpub.com/support.

Piracy

Piracy of copyright material on the Internet is an ongoing problem across all media. At Packt, we take the protection of our copyright and licenses very seriously. If you come across any illegal copies of our works in any form on the Internet, please provide us with the location address or website name immediately, so that we can pursue a remedy.

Please contact us at copyright@packtpub.com with a link to the suspected pirated material.

We appreciate your help in protecting our authors, and our ability to bring you valuable content.

Questions

You can contact us at questions@packtpub.com if you are having a problem with any aspect of this book, and we will do our best to address it.

1
Cacti Overview

Computerization has boosted human intellectual capacity to such a level that a new era of communication has begun. There is hardly any human activity that has not been affected by a computer in one way or another; be it production, agriculture, health, education, military, travel, crime detection, and so on. Naturally, computerization is so deep that we humans can't think of living a single day without it.

In the field of Information Technology, computer communication means networking between computers that can be classified as LAN (Local Area Network), WAN (Wide Area Network), ISDN (Integrated Services Digital Network), and so on. A network is a series of points or nodes interconnected by communication paths. Networks can interconnect with other networks and contain sub-networks. This interconnectivity is done by devices such as routers, switches, hubs, network interface cards (NIC), and so on. In the present infrastructure, devices are very complex, and hard to maintain and monitor, so it is not possible to monitor devices and servers manually at production level.

One of the fundamental jobs of a network administrator is network monitoring. Network monitoring is the process of checking computers, systems, and services that comprise a network. This examination allows a network administrator to maintain a robust network and even improve the network.

You'll never know when a power supply is going to burn out, when a server is going to crash, when network bandwidth drops, when a router just stops working, when your LAN is hacked, and so on. You will never know when these things will happen, but you can be prepared for situations like these. Effective network monitoring will help to cope with such situations and minimize down-time. It will also help to collect periodic information about the network, which will help you to generate log files and performance charts of system capabilities and responses. With such data, you will be able to optimize your network infrastructure and performance.

To do this job effectively, **ISO (International Organization for Standardization)** designed a model called FCAPS to aid in the understanding of the major functions of a network management system:

- Fault management
- Configuration management
- Accounting management
- Performance management
- Security management

By implementing network monitoring software, system administrators can gather sufficient amounts of data and reports periodically, which will help them to perform management processes fairly and more easily. There are several commercial and open source network monitoring software that are robust and one-stop guiding tools. Cacti is one such tool, robust and one of the best!

What is Cacti?

Cacti is an open source, network monitoring and graphing tool written in PHP/MySQL. It uses the RRDTool (Round-robin database tool) engine to store data and generate graphics, and collects periodical data through Net-SNMP (an application suite to implement SNMP—Simple Network Management Protocol).

Ian Berry had started developing Cacti back in June 2001, while he was working with a local Internet service provider in the U.S. He found that RRDTool is flexible enough to generate complex graphing and reports about network infrastructures, but it was lacking a friendly interface. So, he started developing the interface with PHP/MySQL and had the first public release (version 0.6) on November 21, 2001. Soon, the application gained its popularity in the open source community.

In 2004, Ian brought a second developer into the team, which has expanded to six developers today. Here they are (in the order of joining the project):

- Ian Berry
- Larry Adams
- Tony Roman
- J.P. Pasnak
- Jimmy Conner
- Reinhard Scheck

Why Cacti?

First of all, Cacti is an open source tool. Classically, it can graph network bandwidth with SNMP; but a lot of different graphing can be done with SNMP, Perl, or Shell scripts. There are several important reasons why a system administrator should choose Cacti as a network monitoring tool – it is by far the best RRDTool front-end:

- It's easy to install and you don't need to be a guru or spend tons of hours to configure it.
- You don't need a lot of pre-requisite tools.
- It has a very flexible web interface built with PHP/MySQL.
- It has a very active public forum to get support and updates.
- You can share "Cacti templates" with other users on the forum, which will save a lot of time, rather than design all the templates from scratch.
- You can add plug-ins to Cacti and enable integration of other free tools such as Ntop and PHP Weathermap. (We will talk about plug-ins in a later chapter.)

Cacti operation

Cacti operation is divided into three different tasks:

- Data retrieval
- Data storage
- Data presentation

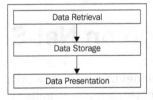

Data retrieval

Cacti retrieves data through poller. It's an application executed at a constant time interval as a schedule service under different operating systems. It is set in the operating system scheduler. In Unix, it is set under crontab.

 Cacti uses cmp.php by default. But if a faster poller is required due to a large infrastructure, then you can use spine, formally known as cactid, a very fast poller written in C that makes use of POSIX threads and links directly to Net-SNMP library for minimal SNMP polling overhead.

Presently, network infrastructure contains lot of different devices such as routers, switches, servers, UPS, and different computer and network appliances. To retrieve data from these remote devices, Cacti use SNMP (Simple Network Management Protocol). Devices that are capable of using SNMP can be monitored by Cacti.

Data storage

There are lot of options to do this task, such as SQL database and flat file database. Cacti uses RRDTool to store data. We will learn more about the RRDTool later in this chapter.

RRD is a system to store and show time series data collected from different SNMP-capable devices. It consolidates historical data based on consolidation functions such as AVERAGE, MINIMUM, MAXIMUM, and so on to keep the storage size minimum. That's why it's fast and easy to create graphs and reports from RRD files.

Data presentation

The most important feature of the RRDTool is a built-in graphing function. Cacti uses this built-in graphing function to deploy customized graphing reports based on time series data collected from different SNMP-capable devices. This built-in graphing function supports auto-scaling and logarithmic y-axis. It is possible to graph one or many items in one graph, also adding different legends denoting characteristics such as maximum, average, minimum, etc.

Basic knowledge on Net-SNMP

In today's complex network of routers, switches, servers, and UPS, it can be a daunting task to manage all the devices on a network and make sure they're not only up and running but also performing optimally. This is where Simple Network Management Protocol (SNMP) can help. SNMP was introduced in 1988 to meet the growing need for a standard for managing Internet Protocol (IP) devices.

Net-SNMP is a suite of software for using and deploying SNMP protocol (version v1, v2c, and v3) and AgentX subagent protocol. It supports IPv4, Ipv6, IPX, AAL5, UNIX domain sockets and others. The suite includes:

- Command line applications
- A generic client library
- A graphical MIB browser using Perl/TK

- A daemon application for receiving SNMP notifications (snmptrapd)
- An extensible SNMP agent to respond to management queries (snmpd)
- Perl, C, and Python modules and sets of APIs to build external applications

The root of the Net-SNMP goes all the way back to 1992; Steve Waldbusser of Carnegie-Mellon University started a freely available SNMP tool kit. Later, Wes Hardaker at University of California Davis took over the project. He extended the agent to provide more information about his local systems (a private precursor to the Host Resources MIB) and to flag certain error situations. He also added a simple way for the agent to run additional scripts and report the results, turning it into an extensible agent. In 1995, this code was made publicly available.

Basic knowledge on RRDtool

RRDTool is a high performance data logging and graphing system, designed to handle time series data like network bandwidth, room temperature, CPU load, server load, and to monitor devices such as routers, UPS, etc. It is also known as the round-robin database tool, an industry standard, open source solution. It lets the administrator log and analyze data collected from all kinds of data sources (DS), which are capable of answering SNMP queries. The data analysis part of the RRDTool is based on the ability to generate graphical representations of the data values collected over a definable time period.

RRDTool is developed by Tobi Oeticker, also known for his famous creation MRTG. RRDTool is written in C language and stores its data in .rdd files. The number of records in a single .rrd file never increases, meaning that old records are frequently removed, and it presents useful graphs by processing the data to enforce a certain data density. RRDTool offers several command line switches to access and manipulate .rdd files:

- create
- update
- updatev
- graph
- dump
- restore
- fetch
- tune
- last

- `info`
- `rrdresize`
- `xport`
- `rrdcgi`

 Details of the command line switches of the RRDTool can be obtained from `http://oss.oetiker.ch/rrdtool/doc/rrdtool.en.html`.

There are also a number of language bindings for RRDTool, which allow administrators or programmers to use it directly from Perl, Python, tcl, PHP, and Ruby. So, it can be used to write custom monitoring shell scripts or create whole applications using its language bindings. Cacti is an application written in PHP, using its PHP language binding.

How does the RRDTool work?

RRDTool follows a logical design to acquire and process data collected from data sources (DS). The following is a brief discussion of the different steps in the logical process:

- **Data acquisition**: When monitoring a device or system, it is necessary to receive data on a constant time interval. Manually, it is not possible to maintain such activity as a system administrator. In such situations, the RRDTool comes in handy. It stores the data in a round-robin database, which is received on a constant time interval set by the system administrator, using the poller application set as scheduler in the operating system.

- **Data consolidation**: The system administrator may log the data in a five-minute interval, but he/she might be interested in knowing the accumulated update over the last month. In this case, simply storing the data in a five-minute interval for the whole month will solve the problem. But this will require huge disk space and a considerable amount of time to analyse the data, as in a network environment, administrators are not monitoring only a single device. RRDTool solves this problem with the data consolidation feature. When creating a round-robin database, the administrator can define at which interval data consolidation should occur using consolidation functions (CF) such as MAXIMUM, AVERAGE, MINIMUM, and others.

- **Round Robin Archives of consolidated data**: Data values of consolidation setup are stored in Round Robin Archives (RRA). In this way, the RRDTool stores data in the most efficient way for a certain time period defined by the system administrator. This process keeps the database file at a constant size for faster processing and analyzing.

- **Unknown data**: RRDTool stores data at a constant interval in a round-robin database. Sometimes, this data might not be available to store in RRD due to device failure or other causes. In this case, the RRDTool stores the RRD file with *UNKNOWN* data value. This *UNKNOWN* value is supported by all RRDTool functions.

- **Graphing**: RRDtool allows system administrator to generate reports in graphical and numerical forms based on data stored in the round-robin database (RDD) by using its built-in graph processing functions. Customization of these graphics is possible based on color, size, and contents.

Summary

Now, we have a basic knowledge about the Cacti application and its operation by using Net-SNMP and the RRDTool. Cacti is a one-stop, web-based solution to monitor network infrastructure and resources. It's easy to use and configure. The most amazing thing about it—you don't need to be an expert Linux administrator to use it. So, let's see how to install Cacti.

2
Prerequisites and Installing Cacti on Linux

In the first chapter, we learned some basic information about Cacti and SNMP. In this chapter, we will install Cacti on our localhost. Cacti runs best on Unix/Linux systems. In this book, all the examples are based on Debian Linux. If you are running a different distribution, you should be able to simply replace `apt-get install` with the appropriate command (`urpmi`, `yum`, and so on), like for centos you have to use `yum install`.

Cacti's prerequisites

Cacti has some prerequisites. You need to install these packages before installing Cacti:

- RRDTool1.0.49 or higher.
- NET-SNMP.
- MySQL4.1.x or higher.
- PHP 4.3.6 or higher.
- Apache/IIS or any other web server.

We will also need to install some other packages for support. Although you can choose to use Apache, IIS, or any other web server, in this book, we will be using Apache2. If you are going to install some other web server, please follow the manual/handbook for that web server.

Installing Cacti prerequisites

The following are methods to install the software required by Cacti to function:

Apache

Open a shell and log-in as root or change to super user (su or sudo -s).

```
$ su
```

This command will ask you for a root password. Suppose our root password is debianserver, type it, and remember that the characters will not be shown on screen.

Now, we are going to install Apache. Type this command on the same terminal:

```
$ apt-get install apache2
```

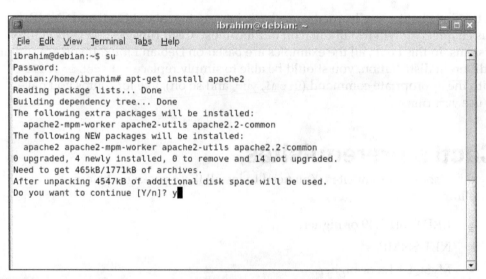

This will install Apache2 with all its dependencies. After that, open http://localhost in your favourite browser.

If everything goes fine, you will see **It Works!** on the top.

> **Using the GUI tool to install packages**
> You can use the Synaptic Package Manager to install these packages.

PHP

Now that our web server is ready, we will install PHP. In the previous shell, type this command:

```
$ apt-get install php5 libapache2-mod-php5
```

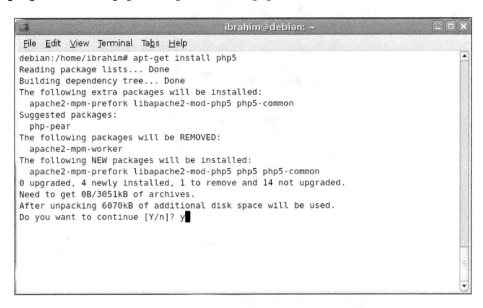

It will install PHP 5 and `libapache2-mod-php5` will configure Apache2 to run PHP scripts. Here, we choose PHP 5 as it's recommended for advance configurations of Cacti. Now, we need to restart the Apache 2 server so that the changes take effect:

```
$/etc/init.d/apache2 restart
```

Now, we need to test PHP to check whether it's working okay or not. So, make `info.php` in the `/var/www/` folder and paste the following PHP code:

```
<?php
    phpinfo();
?>
```

Then, open `http://localhost/info.php` in your browser. If everything goes fine, you will get a page like this:

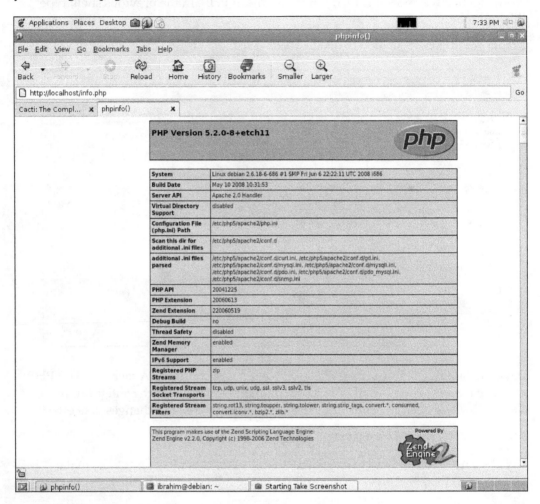

MySQL

MySQL is a database engine that is used by many open source projects. MySQL is used by Cacti for storing setting, user, and display-related information. As MySQL 5 is the stable version, we will be using that version. In the same root shell that you had opened earlier, enter the following command:

```
$ apt-get install mysql-server-5.0 php5-mysql
```

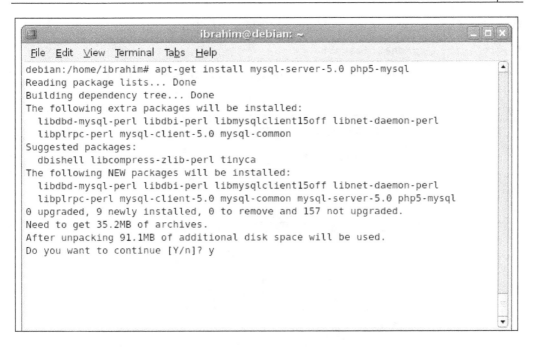

This will install MySQL server version 5 and PHP5-MySQL, which will configure PHP so that it can talk to a MySQL server. A wizard will ask you to enter a password for the MySQL root user (as shown in the following screenshot). You need to be careful here, because it will not ask you to confirm the password, so you have only one chance to do it. Let's set the password as mysqlserver, or whatever you want. And remember it, as we will need this later.

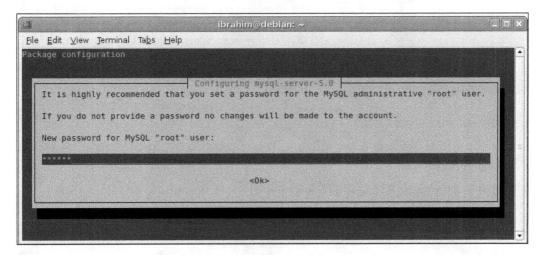

After completing this wizard, we have to restart Apache.

```
$ /etc/init.d/apache2 restart
```

Reload `http://localhost/info.php` and check if PHP has loaded the MySQL module:

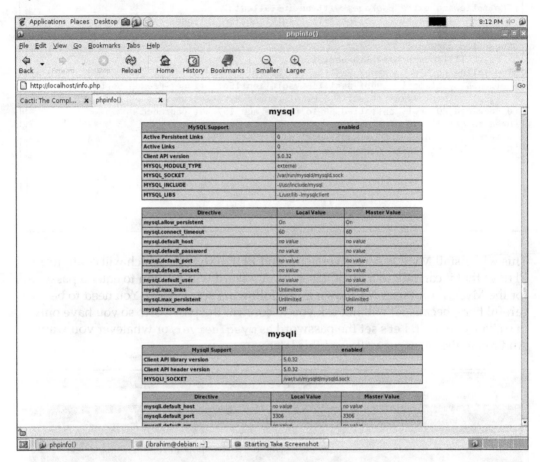

OK, so now we have a LAMP (Linux, Apache, MySQL, PHP) configured system.

Net-SNMP

Next, we need to install Net-SNMP along with the PHP module for Net-SNMP. We can install both by using the same method seen previously:

```
$ apt-get install snmp php5-snmp
```

This will install Net-SNMP and configure PHP to use the Net-SNMP module. After the installation is done, you must restart Apache.

```
$ /etc/init.d/apache2 restart
```

Then, reload `http://localhost/info.php` and check if PHP has loaded the SNMP module.

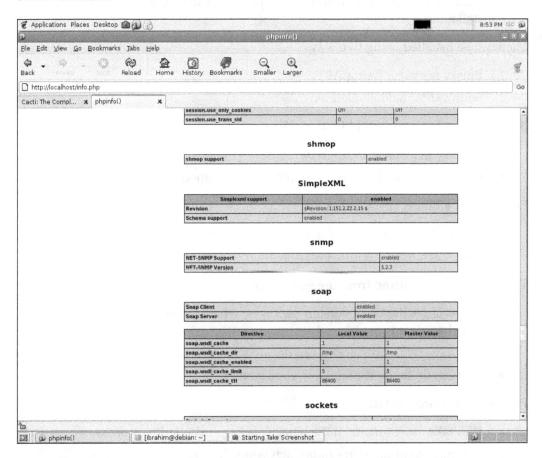

RRDTool

RRDTool is available in the Debian repository, so you can install it through APT.

```
$ apt-get intall rrdtool
```

Installing Cacti

After completing all the commands, we have installed all the dependences for Cacti, and can move on to the Cacti installation.

Ensure that all the previous commands have completed and you have a functioning LAMP server with SNMP and RRDTool support prior to continuing with the Cacti installation.

Cacti can be installed using two ways:

1. Binary package/Using APT.
2. Source/Manual installation.

Benefits of installing from a binary package:

- It's easy to install and upgrade.
- Needs less time than the other installation method.

Problems of a binary installation:

- You will have less control of the installation process.
- Your Cacti maybe a little backdated.

The benefits of installing from the source are:

- You will get the latest version packages, whereas the binary is sometimes little backdated.
- You have total control, you can decide what you need.
- You can do the best tuning for your system.

Problems of source installation:

- Will take more time than the binary package installation process.
- You have to update/upgrade Cacti yourself.
- You may miss an important patch for your Cacti and, this may leave some security holes open.

After reading all these points, you need to decide which installation method suits you best. If you are a new Linux user or have less experience in using Linux, I recommend following the binary method covered in the following section *Installing Cacti using APT*. But if you have enough experience, I recommend the manual installation, for which you can follow the section *Installing Cacti From Source*.

Installing Cacti using APT

In the binary method, you can install through third-party tool or the OS's package manager. Cacti can be installed on Debian server using APT (Debian's package managing tool).

We are going to install Cacti on a Linux machine. Here, we are going to use Debian GNU/Linux version 4 (etch). Debian's package managing tool is APT. Before continuing, be sure that you got no error previously. We are now in the last step of installing Cacti.

```
$ apt-get install cacti
```

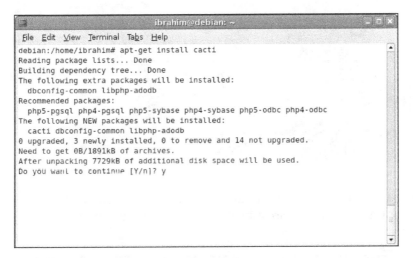

This command will start installation of Cacti. A wizard will start, and ask you some important information. Here, I am going to discuss the details of this procedure:

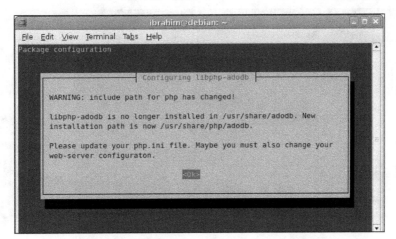

This is simple a warning. You can ignore it. It says libphp-adodb moved to new location.

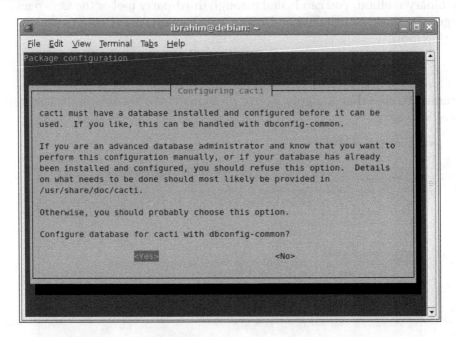

Here, you can decide if you want to take help from debconfig to configure the database for Cacti. If you are not advanced user, then I recommend following this wizard.

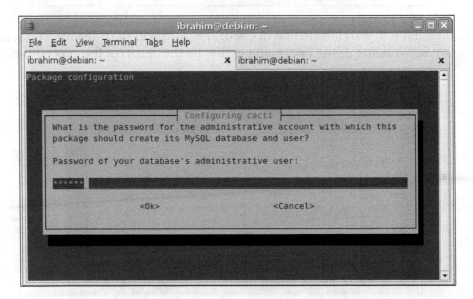

Here, you have to enter the MySQL root password—`mysqlserver`, or whatever you had set before—so that it can create a Cacti user and database on the MySQL server. It will not ask you again for the password confirmation, so you need to little careful here.

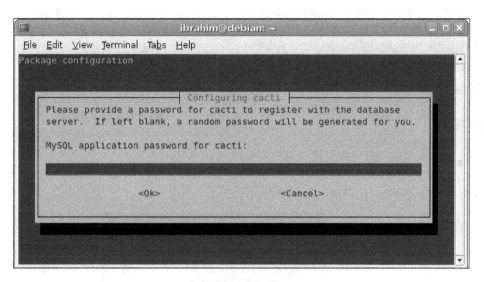

Here, the dialog is asking you to give an input for the Cacti user's password for the MySQL database. After pressing *Enter*, you have to give the same password again for confirmation. Let's set it to `cactiuser` or whatever you want.

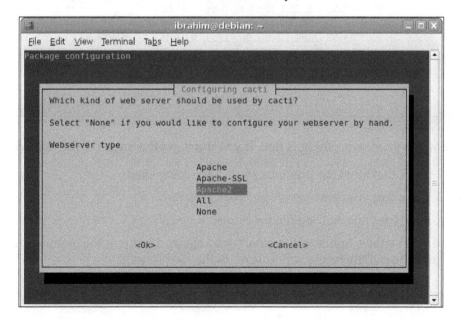

If anything goes wrong or you selected the wrong option, you can start this wizard again using this command:

```
$ dpkg-reconfigure cacti
```

As we are using Apache 2 as our web server, you will have to choose **Apache2** from this menu. After this, we are almost ready to configure Cacti. All the necessary files for Cacti are now installed on your system.

To complete the configuration process, open `http://localhost/cacti` in your favorite browser.

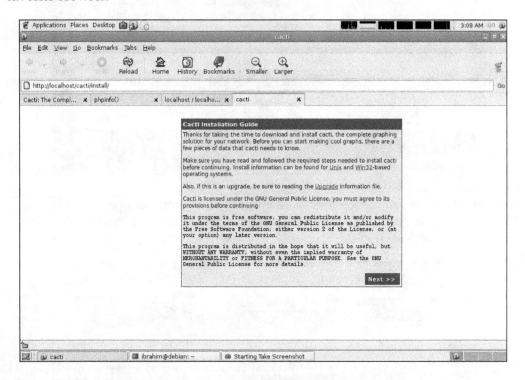

If you got this page, everything is fine. If you don't get this page try the following:

- Ensure that all of the previous steps were completed.
- Ensure that your web server has been restarted.
- Check your apache2 log file for errors.
- If all else fails, uninstall the binary package and jump to the manual install procedure. Otherwise, continue on to the next steps.

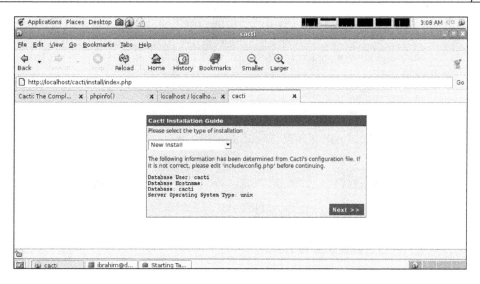

Next is the installation type page. Here, you can select if it's new install or an upgrade. As we are going to install it for the first time, we will select **New Install** (which is selected by default) and click **Next**.

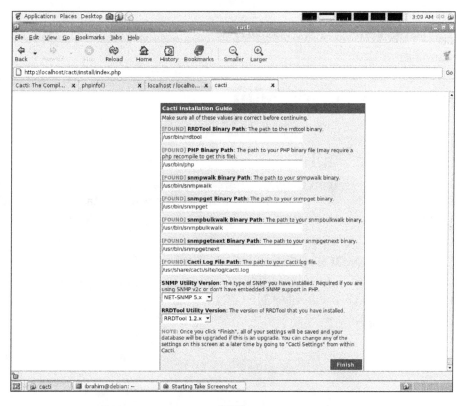

The path settings page automatically determines the installed paths for RRDTool, PHP, SNMP, andCacti.log as well as the versions for Net-SNMP and RRDTool. If any of these are missing, or you want to use a different version, adjust them on this page, and then click **Next**.

RRDTool Binary Path

If you installed RRDTool using APT, the default path is `/usr/bin/rrdtool`.

PHP Binary Path

PHP's default binary path is `/usr/bin/php`.

snmpwalk Binary Path

`/usr/bin/snmpwalk`

snmpget Binary Path

`/usr/bin/snmpget`

snmpbulkwalk Binary Path

`/usr/bin/snmpbulkwalk`

snmpgetnext Binary Path

`/usr/bin/snmpgetnext`

Cacti Log File Path

Cacti's default log file path on Debian is `/usr/share/cacti/site/log/cacti.log`. You can change it to any other place if you want to. The www-data user will need write permissions for that directory.

SNMP Utility Version

You will get the SNMP utility version on the output of phpinfo. Right now, it's Net-SNMP5.2.3, so we will select **NET-SNMP 5.x**.

RRDTool Utility Version

To get the version of the RRDTool that you have installed, type:

```
$ apt-cache policy rrdtool
```

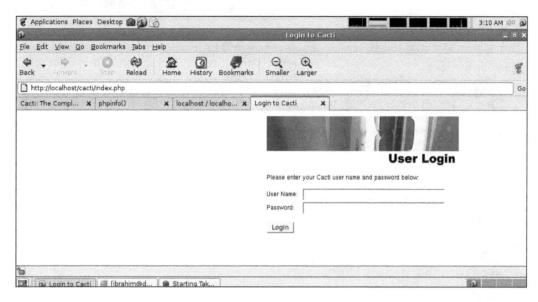

This is Cacti's login screen. The username is `admin` and the default password
is `admin`.

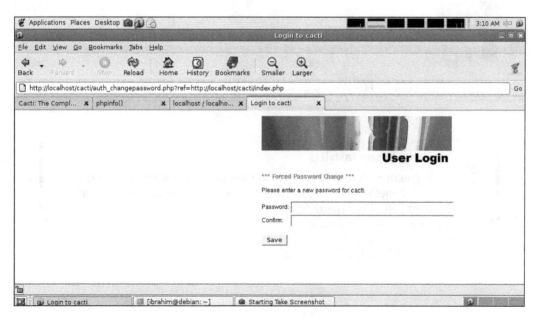

After a successful login for the first time, the system will ask you to set a new password. Enter a new password and ensure you remember it. Without this password, you cannot administer the system!

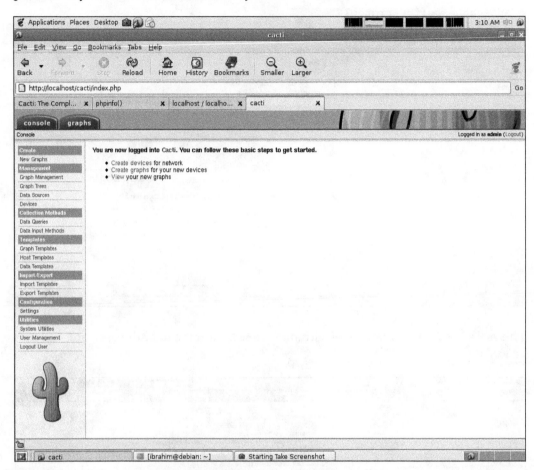

Using binary install

If you don't have a special reason not to, it's better to use the binary install method because it will save you a huge amount of time on both install and upgrade.

Installing Cacti from Source/Manual installation

Here, I will show you how to install Cacti from source.

Though here I am using Debian as my operating system, this procedure will work for most Linux and Unix versions.

Before installing Cacti from source, we must ensure that all its dependency packages are already installed.

1. Download the latest code from the Cacti homepage:

   ```
   $ wget http://www.cacti.net/downloads/cacti-0.8.7b.tar.gz
   ```

2. After completing the download, we have to extract it:

   ```
   $ tar -xzvf cacti-0.8.7b.tar.gz
   ```

3. Now, we will create a new MySQL database called `cacti`.

   ```
   $ mysqladmin -uroot -p create cacti #need password
   ```

4. It will ask for a password for the MySQL root user, enter `mysqlserver` or the MySQL root password that you set previously.

5. Now, we need to import `cacti.sql` to the `cacti` database:

   ```
   $ mysql -uroot -p cacti < cacti-0.8.7b/cacti.sql
   ```

6. So, our database is ready now. Next, we will need to move the downloaded `cacti` folder to the web server's root folder. For Debian, Apache's root folder is `/var/www/`. This will move all the Cacti files and folders to `/var/www`:

   ```
   $ mv cacti-0.8.7b /var/www/cacti
   ```

7. Now, we have to configure Cacti to use the database that we just created:

   ```
   $ cd /var/www/cacti
   $ nano include/config.php
   ```

   In the following code, replace `$database_username` and `$database_pass-word` with your own username and password that you created before.

   ```
   $database_type = "mysql";
   $database_default = "cacti";
   $database_hostname = "localhost";
   $database_username = "cactiuser";
   $database_password = "cactiuser";
   $database_port = "3306";
   ```

It is recommended that you do not use the root user here, instead make a separate MySQL user for this database and give that user permission only to the Cacti database.

```
$ mysql -uroot -p mysql    # will ask you root password
mysql> GRANT ALL ON cacti.* TO cacti@localhost IDENTIFIED BY
"cacti987"
mysql> flush privileges;
```

A new user `cacti` will be created with the password `cacti987`. Now, you have to edit `include/config.php` with this user information. After editing that file, it will look like:

```
$database_type = "mysql";
$database_default = "cacti";
$database_hostname = "localhost";
$database_username = "cacti";
$database_password = "cacti987";
$database_port = "3306";
```

> **Single user per database**
>
>
> It's always a good idea to make a single user account for every user, allowing that user access only from localhost, if you will not be accessing your database from outside your network. For example: the database and the web server are on the same system.

8. Next, we create a cron job that will run `poller.php` every five minutes.

```
$ touch /etc/cron.d/cacti
```

Then, edit the `/etc/cron.d/cacti` with your favorite editor and paste the following text there:

```
*/5 * * * * www-data php /var/www/cacti/poller.php> /dev/null 2>&1
```

This cron will poll the required data and store it in the `rra` folder. We have to change the ownership of `rra` and `log` folder to `www-data`.

```
$ chown -R www-data rra/ log/
```

Now, open `http://localhost/cacti` in your favorite browser.

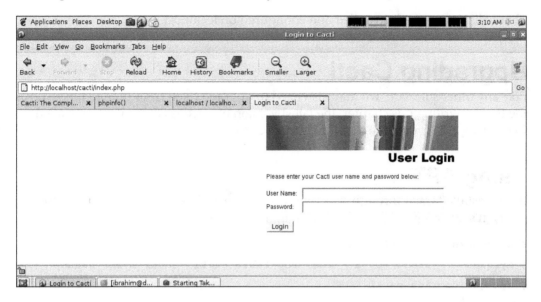

If you get this page, you are done. Now, you can log in using admin as the username. The password is also admin.

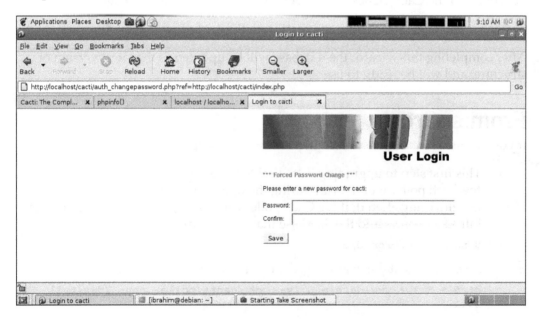

After a successful login for the first time, it will ask you for a new password.

That's all! Your Cacti is installed and configured on localhost.

Upgrading Cacti

Like any other software, we may also need to upgrade Cacti from time to time. At the time of writing this chapter, the latest version of Cacti is 0.8.7b. If you installed Cacti using APT, you have to follow the procedure below.

Using APT

If you installed Cacti through APT, you don't have to do anything special. But for safety, it's always good practice to back up the data before upgrade.

```
$ cp /usr/share/cacti /some/safe/place
$ mysqldump --uroot -p -1 --add-drop-table cacti >cacti_mysql_backup
$ apt-get upgrade cacti
```

After successfully upgrading using APT, you have to visit `http://localhost/cacti/install`. You will get the setup start page (the page you already saw at the time of installing Cacti). Click on the **Next** button to go to the next page.

On the second page, select **Upgrade cacti** from the drop-down menu and click **Next**.

After completing this wizard, the database will be updated to the latest version or structure, and will be ready to use.

From source

If you installed Cacti from source, then follow these steps:

1. This first step to upgrading is to disable the `poller.php` cronjob so that the Cacti poller will not run during the upgrade cycle. Since the database is usually being altered, if the Cacti poller runs during the upgrade cycle, it can introduce errors into the database that can corrupt your setup.

    ```
    $ nano /etc/cron.d/cacti
    ```

    Also, add a # at the beginning. So, the file will now look like:

    ```
    #*/5 * * * * www-data php /var/www/cacti/poller.php> /dev/null 2>&1
    ```

2. Now, we will create a backup of the database:

    ```
    $ mysqldump -uroot -p -1 --add-drop-table cacti >cacti_mysql.dump
    ```

3. We need to download the latest version from Cacti homepage.

    ```
    $ wget http://www.cacti.net/downloads/cacti-version.tar.gz
    ```

4. Let's go to web root folder.

    ```
    $ cd /var/www
    ```

5. Rename `cacti` folder to `cactiold`:

    ```
    $ mv cacti cactiold
    ```

6. Extract the downloaded file to the web server root folder:

    ```
    $ tar -xvzf /address/where/you/downloaded/cact-version.tar.gz
    ```

7. Now, we have to copy the old rra file to this new `cacti` folder

    ```
    $ cp cactiold/rra/* cacti/rra/
    ```

8. Copy scripts from `cactiold`, but here we will only copy those files that are not available on the new Cacti. That's why here we have to use the `-u` switch/option.

    ```
    $ cp -u cactiold/scripts/* cacti/scripts/
    ```

9. Now, we will copy resources from `cactiold`, such as `scripts`, with the subdirectories.

    ```
    $ cp -u -R cactiold/resource/ cacti/resource/
    ```

10. Lastly, we need to change the ownership of the `rra` and `log` folder:

    ```
    $ chown -R www-data cacti/rra/ cacti/log/
    ```

11. Open `http://localhost/cacti` and you will get the setup start page (the page you already saw at the time of installing Cacti). Click on the **Next** button to get to the next page.

    On the second page you have to select **Upgrade cacti** from the drop-down menu.

    After completing this wizard, the database will update to the latest version or structure and will be ready for use.

12. Now it's time to restart the cron:

    ```
    $ nano /etc/cron.d/cacti
    ```

    and remove the leading hash. That's all!

Patch

Patches are the fixes for an existing installation of Cacti. You should always keep a eye on `http://cacti.net/download_patches.php`, so that you are not missing any patches.

First, enter into your `cacti` directory:

```
$ cd /var/www/cacti
```

Then, download the patch from `http://cacti.net/download_patches.php`.

```
$ wget http://www.cacti.net/downloads/patches/0.8.7b/upgrade_from_
086k_fix.patch
```

You have to downloaded all the patches that are available for your version of Cacti.

Now, time to apply the patch:

```
$ patch -p1 -N < upgrade_from_086k_fix.patch
```

Done, your Cacti is ready!

Summary

In this chapter, we learned how to install Cacti on a Linux machine using both APT and a manual installation. We also learned how to upgrade and apply patches to an existing installation.

3
Using Graphs to Manage Networks and Devices

Now that we have a working Cacti environment, we will see how to add network-attached devices in the Cacti system and produce graphs to monitor LAN-sized installations to complex networks with hundreds of devices. It is fairly easy to manage devices through the Cacti web front-end. It provides a fast poller, advance graph templating, and multiple data acquisition methods out of the box, wrapped in an easy to use interface that makes sense to the network administrator.

Creating graphs

If you are familiar with RRDTool, then you know Cacti is designed to harness the power of RRDTool's data storage and graphing functionality. If you are not, don't worry—Cacti will create graphs without extensive configuration input from users. Built-in graph templates will make your life easier, so it is not necessary to understand the functionality of each field to create graphs for network-attached devices. Each graph stores different sets of parameters that control different aspects of each graph. If you want to know more about RRDTool, please visit `http://oss.oetiker.ch/rrdtool/`.

At the time of creating graphs, you will face a bit of a stiff learning curve. Stay on course, it will be over soon and you will be able to create graphs for different devices very quickly. As we discussed in the previous chapters, Cacti can create graphs for any SNMP-enabled, network-attached devices. This can be a switch, router, server, desktop computer, printer, IPS, UPS, and so on. Initially, we will not talk about the custom template and the data-query script development for any SNMP-enabled devices. Instead, we will use the default options in Cacti. In order to build a custom template, we need to understand the SNMP protocol and command-line tools of the Net-SNMP application suite. In Chapter 6, we will discuss the SNMP protocol and the Net-SNMP application suite in detail. Let's create graphs based on the available templates and devices.

Adding a device

Before we add a graph, we need to add a device for which you want to create the graph. In order to do that, click on **Devices** under **Management**. Cacti will open the **Devices** view panel. It will look like this:

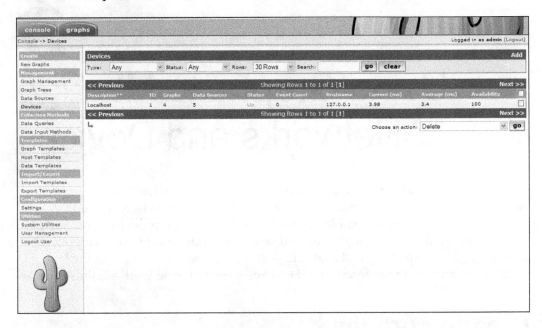

If you click **Add** in the top right-hand corner, it will open a new form to add a new device. The first two fields, **Description** and **Hostname**, are both required for the default configuration. The other fields in the **Device** section (**Notes** and **Disable Device**) can be left as is. If your host template exists in the drop-down, be sure to select the template. Since we are starting with an SNMP-enabled device, if you are not sure which template to select, you can select the **Generic SNMP-enabled host** template. It is important to know that adding a template to a device will not lock down the device to any specific configuration, as graph templates and queries can be added and removed from a device at anytime. The following screenshot shows how the **Add a device** form looks.

If you look closely at the drop-down, there are very few templates. But you can add device-specific templates as required. The following web site has an excellent collection of Cacti scripts and templates. We will discuss templates in greater detail in Chapter 4.

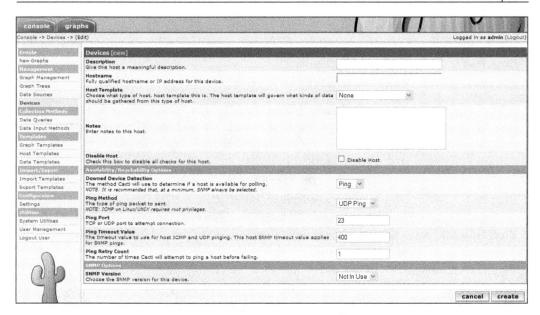

This web site is aimed at providing tips and tricks to Debian users from novice to expert. The owner also collects and updates all sorts of scripts and templates from the Cacti forum for easy access: http://www.debianhelp.co.uk/cactitemplates.htm

Device fields definition

Every device that we add has different attributes and values. The following table will clarify the attributes. It is wise to understand all the fields before adding a device in Cacti.

Field	Description
Description	Giving host a meaningful name. This name will be shown in the first column of the device view panel.
Hostname	Fully qualified hostname or IP. If a fully qualified hostname is being used, such as linuxbox1.example.com, Dynamic Name Services (DNS) will be used to resolve the hostname.
Host Template	Host template is responsible for the types of data that need to be gathered from a specific type of host.
Notes	Adding notes for the host, anything that is specific to the host.
Disable Host	Check this box to disable all the checks for this device. This means no polling for this device.

Fields	Descriptions
Downed Device Detection	NONE: Disable downed device detection. Ping and SNMP: Perform both tests. SNMP: Perform SNMP check. Ping: Use ping method.
Ping Method	ICMP Ping: Perform ICMP test. ICMP on Linux/Unix require root privileges. TCP Ping: Perform a TCP test. UDP Ping: Perform UDP test.
Ping Port	This option is available for only TCP and UDP Ping. Define the port number here and make sure the firewall is not blocking that port.
Ping Timeout Value	This value is measured in milliseconds. After the defined time, the test will fail.
Ping Retry Count	Defines how many times Cacti will ping a host before failing.
SNMP Version	Version 1: Supported by most of the SNMP-enabled devices. One thing you need to remember is that it doesn't support a 64-bit counter. Version 2: This is also known as SNMPv2c. Supported by most of the SNMP-enabled devices. Version 3: Version 3 supports authentication and encryption.
SNMP Community	SNMP read community for the device.
SNMP Port	UDP port number to use for SNMP (default is 161).
SNMP Timeout	Maximum number of milliseconds Cacti will wait for an SNMP response (does not work with PHP-SNMP support).
Maximum OID's Per Get Request	This feature only works when you use the spine poller. Specifes the number of OIDs that can be obtained in a single SNMP get request. This is a performance feature.
SNMP Username (v3)	SNMP v3 username for the device.
SNMP Password (v3)	SNMP v3 password for the device.
SNMP Auth Protocol (v3)	SNMPv3 authorization protocol. There are two options: MD5, which is default, and SHA.
SNMP Privacy Passphrase (v3)	Passphrase specifies privacy when encryption happens for all SNMP packets. You can choose the encryption protocol below.

Fields	Descriptions
SNMP Privacy Protocol (v3)	DES is the default option; you can also use AES. DES means Data Encryption Standard. DES encryption is 56 bits long. AES means Advance Encryption Standard. AES keys can be 128, 192, or 256 bits long.
SNMP Context	SNMP Context needs to be used when the same OID tree is proxied to multiple devices. When using View-Based Access Control Model (VACM), it is possible to specify an SNMP Context when mapping a community name to a security name with a com2sec directive, with the group directive and the access directive. This allows defining special access models.

I have used following information for the device, which is a computer running Cacti:

- **Description**: CactiBox
- **Hostname**: 192.168.59.128
- **Host Template**: Local Linux Machine
- **Downed Device Detection**: Ping and SNMP
- **Ping Method**: UDP Ping
- **Ping Port**: 23
- **Ping Timeout Value**: 400
- **Ping Retry Count**: 1
- **SNMP Version**: Version 2
- **SNMP Community**: Public
- **SNMP Port**: 161
- **SNMP Timeout**: 500
- **Maximum OID's Per Get Request**: 10 (this performance function does not work if you don't use the spine poller).

After creating the device, Cacti redirects you to the same form with additional information. If it is successful, a successful information screen will be shown:

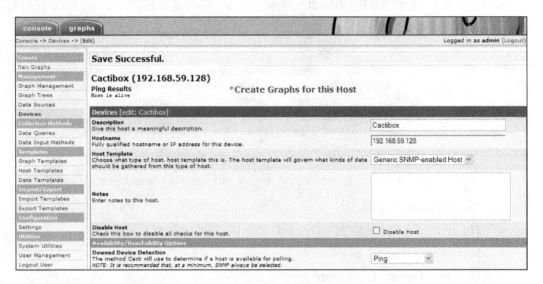

If you see an SNMP error, there is a SNMP problem between the device running Cacti and the device you are attempting to graph.

You can use snmpwalk in the command line to debug the issue. The following command will print interface table. Before using snmpwalk, check whether snmpd is running or not and that it is configured to listen from other interfaces.

```
snmpwalk -v 2c -c public 192.168.59.128 sysUpTimeInstance
```

If the SNMP implementation is working on your machine, you will see an output like the following (I have just shown one portion of the output):

```
DISMAN-EVENT-MIB::sysUpTimeInstance = Timeticks: (13072) 0:02:10.72
```

For further information on snmpwalk please visit the following web site http://www.net-snmp.org/docs/man/snmpwalk.html

At the bottom of the previous image, you will see two more options:

- **Associated Graph Templates**
- **Associated Data Queries**

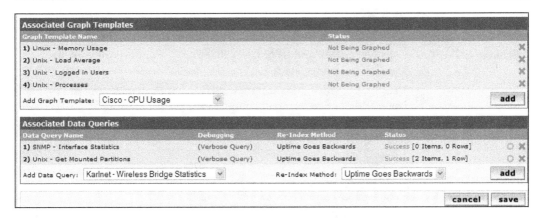

If you have selected host template in the previous page, then you may see a few items in both sections. If you didn't select a host template, you will not see any items in either section. In order to create a graph in the next step, it is best to have at least one item in the **Associated Graph Templates** or **Associated Data Queries**. If you don't have the right template for the host device, please consult the Cacti template repository.

 Cacti template repository — `http://www.debianhelp.co.uk/ cactitemplates.htm`. (We will discuss details about the templates in Chapter 4.)

SNMP support in Cacti

Simple Network Management Protocol (SNMP) is an application layer protocol, which processes the exchange of management information between devices. It is a part of the transmission control protocol suite (TCP/IP). SNMP helps the network administrator to manage network performance, find and solve network problems, and plan for network growth. Three versions of SNMP exist: SNMP version 1 (SNMPv1), SNMP version 2 (SNMPv2c), and SNMP version 3 (SNMPv3). How SNMP will work with your Cacti installation depends on which version you choose. Version 1 is limited on most devices, and should be avoided unless you have no other option. If you want access to greater resources (for example, implement high-speed counter (64bits)) then you can choose version 2. For secure and authenticated implementation, you can choose SNMPv3. Cacti has implemented version 3 fully from 0.8.7 version onwards. The Cacti Group recommends version 2c for ease of use and general support.

Type	Description	Supported Option
External SNMP	Calls Net-SNMP and its binaries that are installed on your system	Supports all versions
Internal SNMP	Uses PHP's SNMP function that calls Net-SNMP or ucd-snmp at compile time	Supports version 1
Spine SNMP	Links directly against usd-snmp or Net-SNMP and calls API	Supports all versions

Creating a graph for the device

Now that we have created a device in the system, it is time to create some graphs for this device. You can jump to creating a graph from two different places: select **New Graphs** under **Create** or if you are still in editing mode of the device, click **Create Graph for this Host**. After clicking the option, you can see a form like the following. You might have different options based on which device/host you choose from the drop-down box.

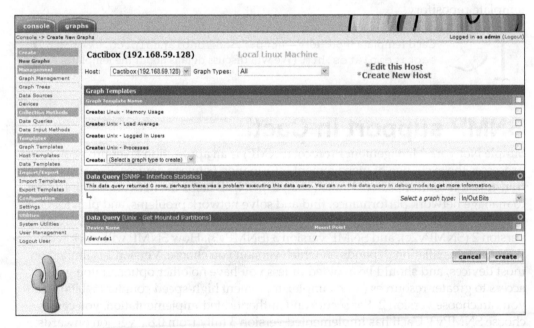

In this example, I am creating a graph for the CactiBox itself. So, you are not seeing some options in the Data Query section. We will see that section when we create a graph for a network interface. It's pretty much straight forward to create a graph for a device. You just need to check the option next to different rows that are shown in the Graph Templates and Data Query sections. After checking the options, click on the **Create** button. You will see another form where you can choose **Legend Color** and some additional options, if the templates require additional input. After inputting the required values in this page, press the **Create** button again to create the graphs. Cacti will then schedule the creation of graphs for the device.

Organizing graphs

In Cacti, graphs can be organized in a hierarchical tree structure. Each graph tree contains zero or more branches containing either hosts or individual graphs. Even each node of the tree could have multiple branches. In this way, we can organize graphs functionally.

You can access **Graph Trees** under **Management**. In the **Graph Trees** page, click on the **add** button for a new graph tree.

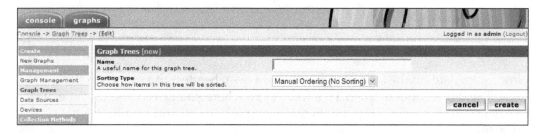

Choose a name and select a sorting type from the drop-down box. There are four sorting types in the drop-down box:

- **Manual Ordering**: Each graph/device that is added can be re-ordered within the tree/branch
- **Alphabetic Ordering**: Each graph/device is ordered alphabetically
- **Numeric Ordering**: Each graph/device is ordered numerically
- **Natural Ordering**: Alphanumeric ordering taking into account numeric increasing

You can choose the sorting that will fit your requirements

In this example, I use a tree name **LinuxBox 192.168.59.128** and sorting type
Manual Ordering.

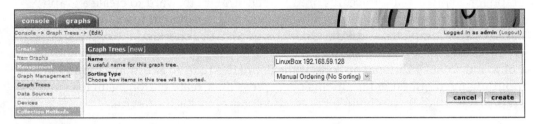

If we click on **Graph Trees** under **Management**, we can see **LinuxBox 192.168.59.128**.
Click on **Linux 192.168.59.128** to add graphs to the tree.

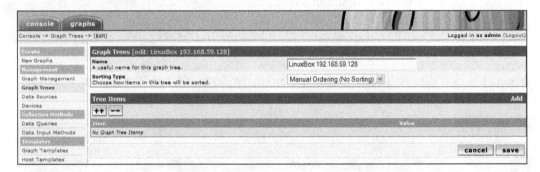

Now, press **Add** on the following page to add host, header, and graphs to the
node. There is an option called **Tree Item Type** where you can choose the type of
tree item — host, header, or graph. In this example, we will add host first, which
is Cactibox.

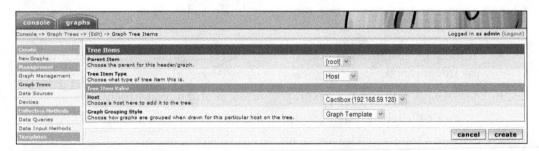

Now, we will add two headers called **Server Stuff** and **Server Traffic**. When it is done, we will add graphs to both headers. In order to do that, click **Add** and the following screen will appear.

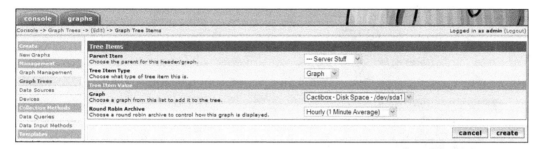

In the **Parent Item** drop-down box, select **Server Stuff**, **graph** in **Tree Item Type**, **Cactibox – Disk Space – /dev/sda1** in **Graph**, and **Hourly (1 Minute Average)** in **Round Robin Archive**. In the same way, add the following graphs under **Server Stuff**:

- **Load Average**
- **Logged in Users**
- **Memory Usage**
- **Processes**

At the end, add Traffic under **Server Traffic**. When you are done, the **LinuxBox 192.168.59.128** graph tree will look like the following image.

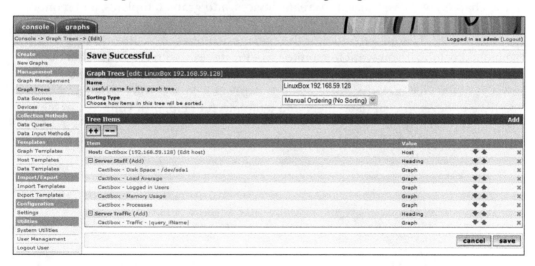

Now, I can see the graphs like the following one by clicking the **Graphs** tab at the top. In order to show the graphs in three columns, I have changed some settings. I will come back to the preview setting in Chapter 8.

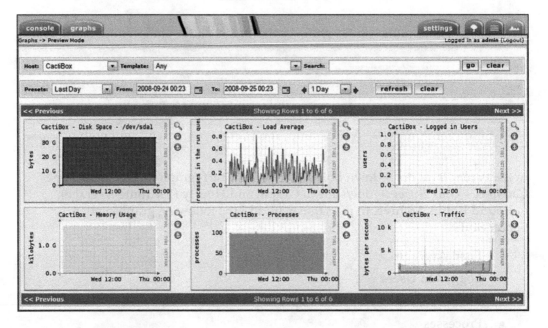

Summary

In this chapter, we have learned to create devices, add graph templates, and monitor network-attached devices. Though we have used built-in templates and data-queries, they are powerful enough to monitor the average activities of a network. As I mentioned before, if you want to monitor specific devices with a specific data query, please consult the Cacti template repository. You can find a complete list of templates at http://www.debianhelp.co.uk/cactitemplates.htm. If you can not find one, you have to develop your data-query and template; for help, post your requirement to the Cacti official forum.

4
Creating and Using Templates

Cacti stores all collected information via RRDTool into files called **rra**. The RRDTool requires some parameters in order to create these rra files. Whenever we want to add a new device or create a new graph, we have to input these parameters. Inputting these parameters manually is flexible, but not very user friendly, and there is always a chance of error. Using templates, we can easily overcome this problem.

For example, let's say we have a network of four Linux servers, two Unix servers, and one Cisco router. Here, if we use a template, we will need to make only three different templates: one for the Linux servers, one for the Unix servers, and one for the Cisco router. You may ask why we have to make a template for the Cisco router? We will make it so that we can use it later.

Cacti templates can be imported and exported via the Console under **Import/Export**. You can only import templates that have been created on a system that is at the same, or an earlier, version of Cacti.

 At the end of this chapter, there is a list of third-party templates that can be imported.

In this chapter, we will learn how to:

- Use/add templates
- Make our own custom templates
- Import templates
- Export templates

Types of Cacti templates

Cacti templates are broken into two areas:

1. Graph templates
2. Host templates

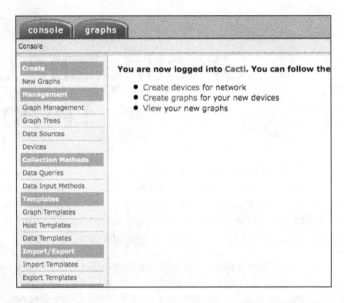

In the above figure, under the **Templates** section, you will see the three types of templates that come with the Cacti basic installation. If you click on one of those links, you will get the complete list of templates for that type.

Graph templates

Graphs are used to visualize the data you have collected. A graph template provides a skeleton for an actual graph. When you have more then one system/device, a graph template will save you lots of time and also reduce the possibility of error. Any parameters defined within a graph template are copied to all the graphs that are created using this template.

Creating a graph template

Now, we are going to create a new graph template. Under the **Templates** heading, click on **Graph Templates**. A list of the already available graph templates will be shown. Click on the **Add** link in the top right corner. You will get a screen like this:

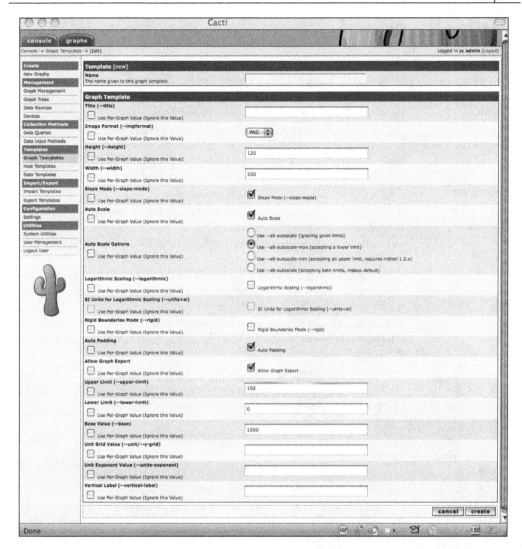

Here, you have to give the values that will be used in future to create the graph.

Field name	Description
Name	Here, you have to input the template name. It can be anything, but it's always a good idea to have a relevant name.
Title (--title)	This title will be displayed on the top of the graph. So, we need to be careful here. The most used and popular title format is | *host_description* | - *your graph name*.
	Here, | *host_description* | is Cacti's own keyword. At the time of creating the graph, Cacti will replace this keyword with the hostname.

Field name	Description
Image Format	The type of image that will be generated; the default, PNG, is fine for almost everyone. There are other two options, SVG and GIF.
Height	Height of the graph. The default value is 120 pixels, which is good enough for all graphs.
Width	Width of the graph. The default value is 500 pixels.
Slope Mode (--slope-mode)	RRDtool graphs are composed of staircase curves by default. This is in line with the way RRDtool calculates its data. Some people favor a more "organic" look for their graphs. RRDTool version 1.2 and above support smoothing of graphs, known as slope mode.
Auto Scale	Check this if you want the graph auto-scaled.
Auto Scale Options	If you checked **Auto Scale**, then you have to select one option from these four. Otherwise, ignore it. **--alt-autoscale (ignoring given limits)** : Here, RRDTool will ignore all the given limits. **--alt-autoscale-max (accepting a lower limit)** : It will accept the lower limit, but the max value will be generated automatically, depending on the stored data. **--alt-autoscale-min (accepting an upper limit)** : Same as the **alt-autoscale-max** except that it accepts the upper limit. (It requires RRDTool 1.2.x.) **--alt-autoscale (accepting both limits):** This accepts both upper and lower limits.
Logarithmic Scaling	Choose this if you want logarithmic y-axis scaling.
SI Units for Logarithmic Scaling	This depends on **Logarithmic Scaling**, so if you haven't checked that you can ignore it.
Rigid Boundaries Mode	From the RRDTool manual, "Normally rrdgraph will automatically expand the lower and upper limit if the graph contains a value outside the valid range. With this option you can disable this behavior." If you don't really need it, you'd better leave it.
Auto Padding	Check this if you want to enable auto-padding in this template.
Allow Graph Export	You have to check this if you want to allow export from this graph template.
Upper Limit	The maximum value that will be displayed on the y-axis. This value is ignored when auto-scaling is turned on.
Lower Limit	The minimum value that will be displayed on the y-axis. This value is ignored when auto-scaling is turned on.
Base Value	Whether you want to base the y-axis labels on 1000 or 1024. This field will typically be set to 1024 for memory and 1000 for traffic measurements.
Unit Grid Value	Sets the unit value for the y-axis.

Field name	Description
Unit Exponent Value	Sets the 10^e scaling of the y-axis. Valid values for this field are between -18 and 18. For example, you could use 3 to display everything in **k** (kilo) or -6 to display everything in **u** (micro).
Vertical Label	The text to print on the left edge of the graph. Usually, it is the units the data on the graph is measured in.

If you have checked **Use Per-Graph Value (Ignore this Value)**, then every time while using this graph template to create a graph, you have to give an input for this option. It's always best to enable this option for title field.

After filling all these fields, click on the **Create** button. The graph template will be created.

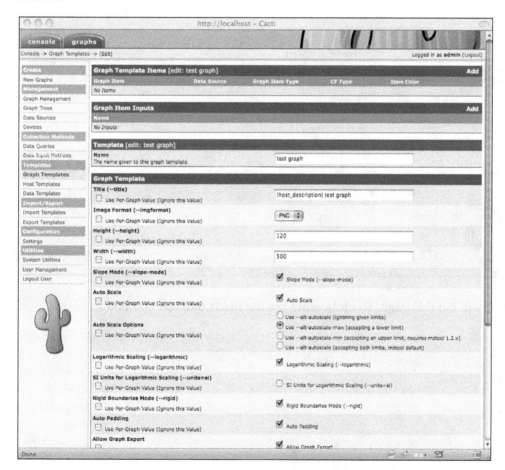

Now, we need to add a **Graph Template Item** and **Graph Item Inputs** to complete this graph template.

Graph Template Item

Graph template items are the various items that will be shown on the graph.

To add a graph template item, click on **Add** on the right side of the **Graph Template Items** box.

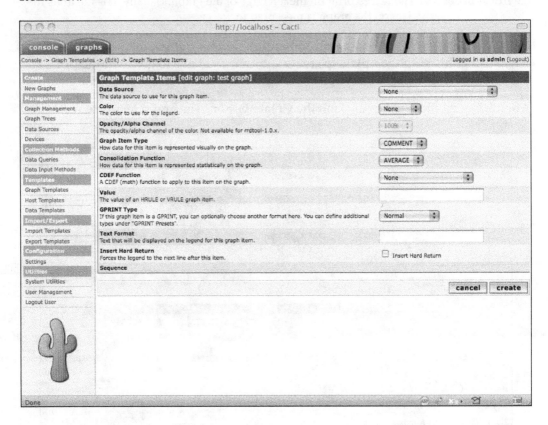

You will get this page. The following are the fields that can be filled in:

Field name	Description
Data Source	The data source to use for this graph item. Select the data source that you want to show on this graph item from the drop-down menu. All graph items may not have a data source. If you don't need any data source for this item, select **None**.
Color	Select the color that you want to use for this data source. It will only be enabled for graph item type LINE1 – LINE3, AREA, and STACK.
Opacity/Alpha Channel	The opacity/alpha channel of the color. Not available for RRDTool-1.0.x.
Graph Item Type	One of the most important fields. Here, you have to select how the data of this item will be shown on the graph. Possible types are: COMMENT, HRULE, VRULE, LINE1-3, Area, Stack, GPRINT, and LEGEND.
Consolidation Function	Here, you have to tell the RRDTool which consolidation function to use. In most of the cases, AVERAGE is used. You may also use MAX, MIN, or LAST for GPRINT items.
CDEF Function	If you want to apply a CDEF function to the graph item, select one here. Check out the CDEF section of the manual for more information.
Value	This field is only used with the HRULE/VRULE graph item types. Type any valid integer to draw the line at for HRULE or the time of day HH:MM for VRULE.
GPRINT Type	If this item is a GPRINT, you can choose how you want the number to be formatted. You can add your own in the GPRINT Presets section of Cacti.
Text Format	You can enter text to be displayed on the legend here. This field is applicable for all graph item types except for the virtual LEGEND type.
Insert Hard Return	Check this box to force graph items onto the next line.

 When creating a graph item, you must always start with an AREA item before using STACK; otherwise, your graph will not render.

Graph Item Inputs

The second box is **Graph Item Inputs**. Graph item inputs are the input source through which the data will be collected. To add a new graph item input, click on the **Add** link on the right side of the **Graph Item Inputs** box.

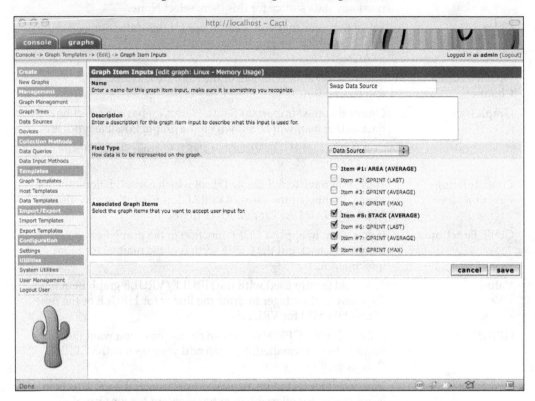

Below are the various fields that have to be filled out for a graph input item:

Fields	Description
Name	This will be used as the identifier for this graph item input on both the graph template and the graph edit page.
Description	It will be displayed on the graph edit page. This field is optional.
Field Type	Here, you have to choose the field that you are going to associate with one or more graph items.
Associated Graph Items	Select the graph items that you want to accept the user input for.

After completing all these fields, click on the **Create** button. Do this again to add more graph item inputs to this graph template.

Host templates

Host templates are a little bit different from data templates and graph templates. A host template is the collection of associated graph templates and data queries that you want associated with a specific host type. As an example, for your localhost, you can use the **Local Linux Machine**. Click on **Host Template** in **Templates** section. You will get the list of host templates that comes with Cacti in the default installation. Let's open the **Local Linux Machine**.

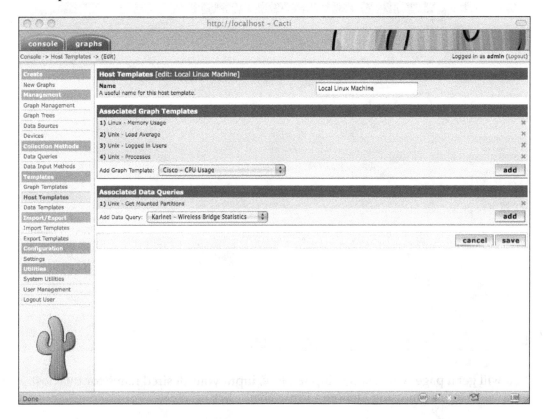

As we can see, it has four associated graphs and one data query. When adding a new device, if we select **Local Linux Machine** as the host template, then all these associated graph and data query templates will be added to this device. Host templates are very useful for large networks with lots of devices of the same type.

 These templates will only be associated, letting you quickly create these types of graphs from the host; it will not automatically create the graphs when you add a new host!

Creating host templates

Creating a new host template is very simple. First, click on **New** in the top right corner.

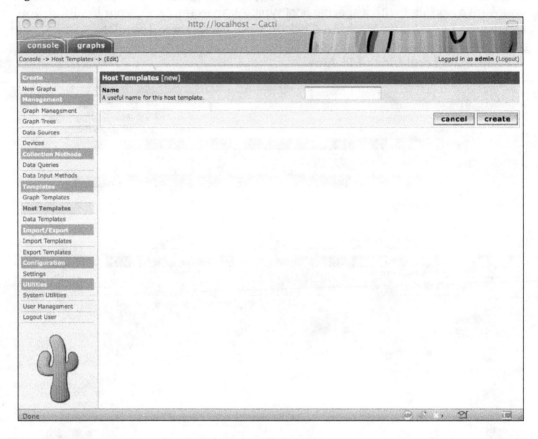

You will get a page with a single input. Now, input your desired name for this host template. Here, I am using **Debian Linux**. Then, click on **create**.

The host template will be created with your desired name. It will look like this:

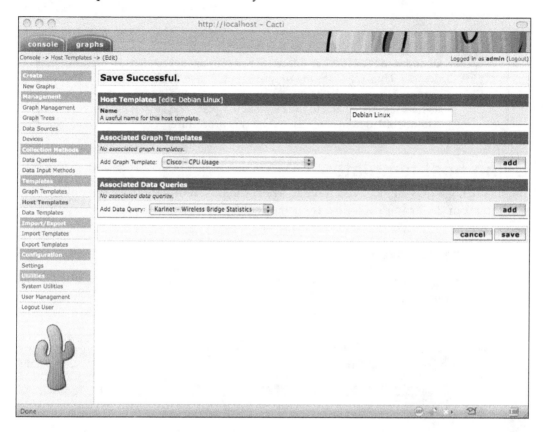

Our new template has been created successfully. Now, we need to add the associated graph templates and data queries.

To add a graph template, select your desired graph template from the drop-down menu and click **Add**. Do it again and again to add other graph templates. In this list, you will also see those graph templates that you made yourself.

To add a data query, select it from drop-down menu and click **Add**. Only add the queries you would normally want for that device type.

After adding all the associated graph templates and data queries, click on **Save**. The host template will be updated and you will see it on the **Host Template** list. It's ready for use on any device.

You can also edit the listed host template to add or remove a graph template and data query.

>
> **Remember!**
> Changes to the Host Template are not propagated to already existing devices. These changes are only applied to new devices. To adjust a current device, set its host template to **None**, save it, and then change its host template back to the original template and save it again. Attention! No items are deleted by this procedure.

Using host templates

When adding a new device, you have to select the host template from the device section. From the drop-down **host template**, select your host template.

Importing templates

At the beginning of this chapter, I told you that Cacti allows for importing and exporting of templates. This allows for the sharing of various templates between the users of Cacti or between your own installations.

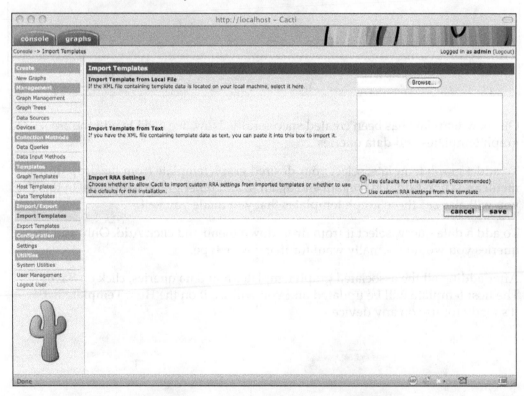

This is the Template Imports page. In Cacti, you can import templates in two ways:

1. From a local file.
2. As pasted text.

Before importing templates into your Cacti installation, you must have a template that you want to import. At the end of this chapter, I will give you a small list of templates that may be helpful for your network.

To import a template from a local file, click on **Browse** and select the file. If you are going to import from text, then paste the text in the input box. Now, if you want to use RRA settings from your installed system instead of the imported template, select **Use defaults for this installation**. Otherwise, select the other option, then the RRA setting will take from the imported template. (It is recommended that you use the first option, unless you are aware of the impacts of the second.)

Now, click on the **save** button. If everything goes fine, you will get a page like this:

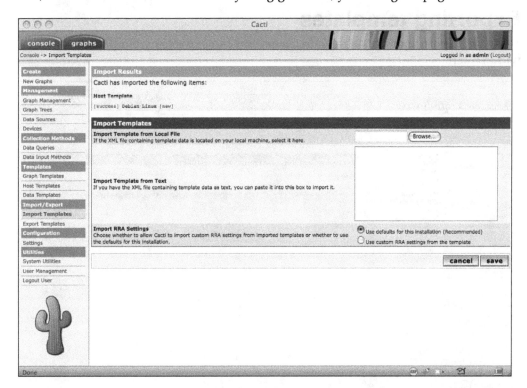

Cacti will indicate if the template is imported successfully or not.

If it's a single OID-based template, you are done. Otherwise, you have to do a couple more steps.

For script-based templates, you have to copy the script that the template author distributed to the `/path/to/cacti/scripts` folder.

For SNMP data queries with an additional XML file holding the data query definition, you have to copy the XML file to the `/path/to/cacti/resources/snmp_queries` folder.

For Script data queries with an additional XML file holding the data query definition, you have to copy the XML file to the `/path/to/cacti/resources/script_queries` folder.

When importing the template, Cacti checks the version of Cacti that exported the template. Your Cacti version has to be equal or higher to import the template successfully; if your Cacti version is 0.8.7a, you cannot import a template that was created with 0.8.7b. You either have to upgrade your version, or find a template that was exported from 0.8.7a.

Exporting templates

Template exporting is very simple in Cacti. You can export any template within Cacti.

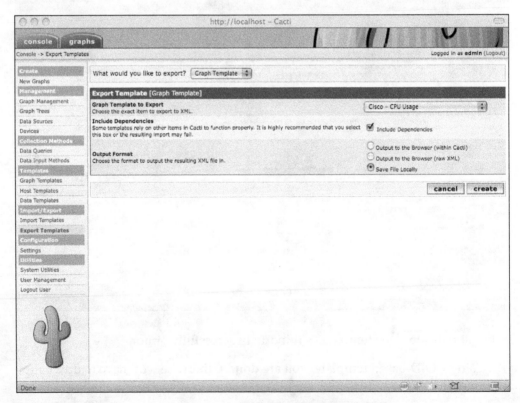

This is the default look of the Template Export page. At the top of the page, you can select what kind of template you are going to export. Possible values are:

1. Graph template
2. Data template
3. Host template
4. Data query

From the drop-down menu, select the template that you want to export. Now, select **Include Dependencies** if you want to also export all the dependent templates, graphs, and so on.

You can export the template in three modes:

1. **Output to the Browser** (within Cacti): Cacti will display the export XML within a Cacti window.
2. **Output to the Browser** (raw XML): Here, the template will be displayed on browser but as raw XML.
3. **Save File Locally**: Here, the exported template will be saved as a file. This is the recommended option if you want to share the template with others.

Now, click **create**. If you chose **Output to the Browser**, just copy the XML from the browser window. For **Save File Locally**, the browser will ask you where you want to save this file.

Important templates

Cacti users are a very friendly bunch. They have already created hundreds of templates for various different devices and graphs. A couple of useful templates that you can download are:

1. Apache stats Template: `http://forums.cacti.net/about9861.html` — useful for web server.
2. MySQL Stats Template: `http://forums.cacti.net/about11010.html`.
3. Graph templates for Squid: `http://forums.cacti.net/about4142.html`.
4. Windows uptime statistics: `http://forums.cacti.net/about10514.html`.

You will get lots of templates at the following URL:
`http://forums.cacti.net/viewtopic.php?t=15067`.

Summary

In this chapter, we learned about templates. Now, you can create or edit a graph template and host template. It's always a good practice to test every template locally before adding it to a production server. Also, we learned to how to import and export Cacti templates.

5
User Management

In this chapter, we will talk about user management. As Cacti offers sophisticated mechanisms for the creation of graphs, its user management mechanism, which provides functionalities to add, edit, and delete users who will be able to create or view graphs and access different areas of Cacti, is equally sophisticated. When Cacti is used in a production environment, it is very important to maintain the access of information. Cacti offers two levels of permission control, realm permissions and graphs permissions, which allow the administrator to control what the user can access, see, and change.

User Management console

If you click on **User Management** under **Utilities**, the **User Management** console will open. It will look more or less like the following:

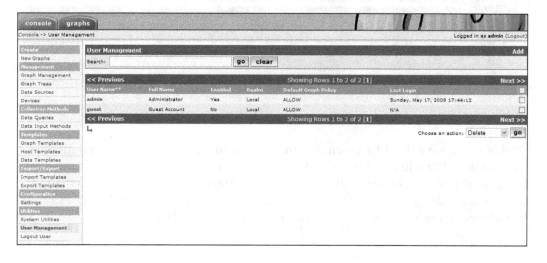

By default, Cacti comes with two users. One is **admin** and another is **guest**. The **admin** user has complete access to the Cacti system. The **guest** user only has view access by default and is an unauthenticated user. This unauthenticated user can only visit graph_view.php and view graphs by default, but can not change graphs. It is best practice to disable access for unauthenticated users in a production environment. By default, in version 0.8.7 and later, the **guest** user is disabled.

Adding a user in Cacti

Now, we will add a user in the Cacti system. It is a fairly easy process and does not take long. We will follow a simple procedure to add a user in the Cacti system. If you click on the **Add** link on the top right hand corner of the **User Management** screen, a new input form like the following will open to create a new user.

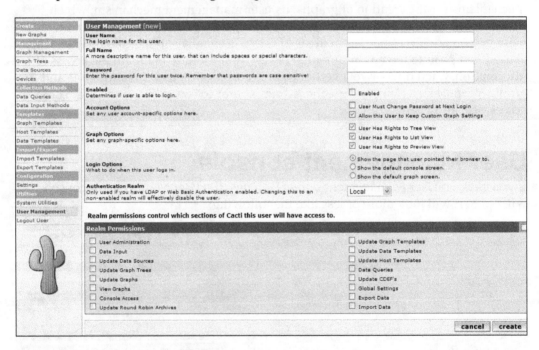

At this point, we will add a username and password and press the **create** button to create a user. We will not think about permissions and other options at this moment. In a production environment, the administrator assigns permissions while creating users. We are doing this to understand the user creation process clearly. For example, let's choose a user called **westwing** with the password **abc123**.

One thing a system administrator must remember while dealing with user accounts is that proper planning is very much necessary before creating user accounts. Cacti does not support groups at this moment. So, it is important to have an option to mass update users. We can do this using Batch Copy. We will talk about Batch Copy later in this chapter.

Editing a user

If we click **User Management**, we can see a list of users on the screen. We can also see the user **westwing**. Now, we will click on **westwing** to edit the user details and permissions. We see a screen like the following:

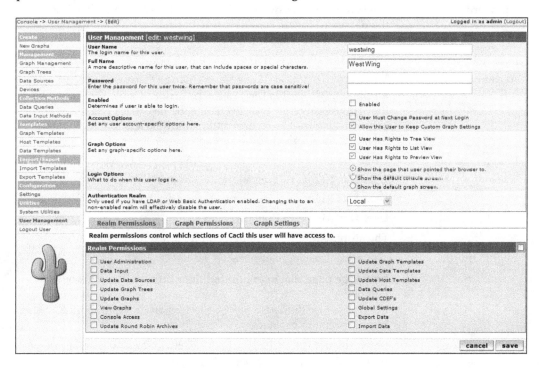

You will see different user-specific options. As the minimum requirements for creating a user are **User Name** and **Password**, the **User Name** field will always be filled out (the password field will appear blank, although it has been set). The following table has other information that may be filled out.

Name	Description
User Name	This is the login name for the user. This username will be used to log in to the Cacti system. There is no character limit in the field but it's better to keep it simple and user friendly.
Full Name	This is an optional field. It is only used to display the full name of the user on the User Management page.
Password	Insert the same password twice in both boxes. Remember that the password is case sensitive. If both boxes are left blank, the password will remain unchanged.
Enabled	This option allows you to disable a user account temporarily.
Account Options	There are two options: **User Must Change Password at Next Login** and **Allow this User to Keep Custom Graph Settings**. The first option forces the user to change the password when new users first log in. The second option allows users to maintain their own custom graph viewing settings.
Graph Options	There are three custom settings for the graph options: **User Has Rights to Tree View** **User Has Rights to List View** **User Has Rights to Preview View** The administrator can change graph view information for users.
Login Options	There are three login options: **Show the page that user pointed their browser to** – This option will take the user to the page where the user was, before being interrupted by the Login box due to session time expiry or a browser-related problem. **Show the default console screen** – This option always takes the users to the index.php page after login. **Show the default graph screen** – This option always takes the users to the graph_view.php page after login.
Authentication Realm	In a large network, different users exist. These settings allow different users to access Cacti. There are three settings — **Local**, **Web Basic**, and **LDAP**. Template users must be Local.

Realm permissions

This section controls which sections of Cacti a respective user can access. If a user is opened in editing mode, **Realm Permission** can be seen at the bottom of the page. Here, users with the **User Administration** realm (usually an administrator) can set and change all the permission for the users. If the administrator wants to offer graph viewing only, then the **View Graph** needs to be checked (the rest of the options would remain unchecked).

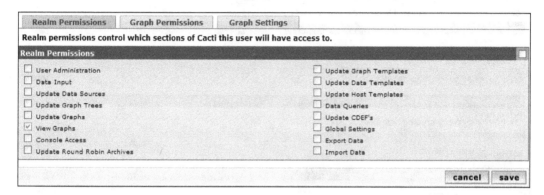

Graph permissions

This section controls which graphs, devices, templates, and trees users can view. If you can master Cacti graph permission combinations, you can produce very complex results in terms of permissions. Permissions are controlled by four options:

- **By Graph**
- **By Device**
- **By Graph Template**
- **By Tree**

The most important thing to remember is policy order, which starts as — **By Graph**, **By Device**, and then **By Graph Template**. Graph policies will be evaluated in the order shown until a match is found. So, if a user has permissions set to **Deny** for a specific graph but **Allow** for **By Device** and **By Graph Template**, the user will not be able to see the graph, because the **By Graph** policy is denied by the Cacti system first according to the policy order.

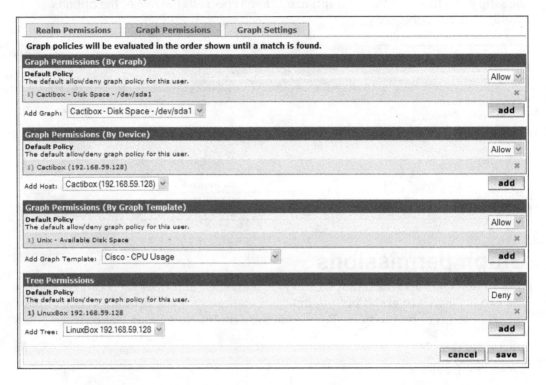

It is recommended that you simply start by placing graphs or devices that a user requires in a specific tree, change the tree default permission to 'Deny' (leaving all others at Allow) and allow that user access to only that specific tree.

 In order to ensure that the user cannot view graphs by other methods, **User Has Rights to Tree View** should be checked and **User Has Rights to List View** and **User Has Rights to Preview View** should be unchecked.

Graph settings

This section allows the administrator to control a user's graph viewing settings (to allow a user to control this themselves, put a check beside **Allow this User to Keep Custom Graph Settings** under **Account Options**). It controls graph view mode, graph size, and fonts. If a user accesses this section and pays close attention, they will be able to adjust how the graphs and trees are presented. If you don't have permission for this section, then you will get the **Access Denied** notice box.

Other User Management options

Now, we will focus on the other options of user management such as:

- **Delete**
- **Copy**
- **Enable**
- **Disable**
- **Batch Copy**

These options can be found in the Choose an action drop-down list, as shown below.

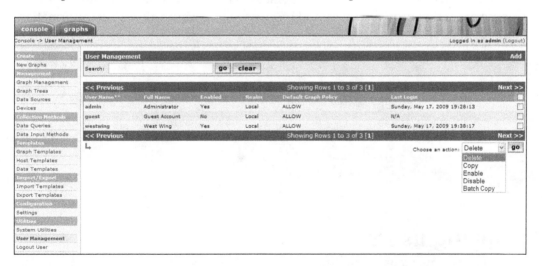

Deleting users

Deleting a single user or several selected users is a straight-forward process within Cacti. Select the user or users from the **User Management** list and select **Delete** from the **Choose an Action** list and press **go**. The system will ask for confirmation. If you press **Yes**, the system will delete the accounts and any stored settings for the user(s).

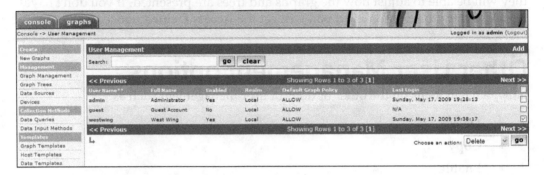

Enabling and disabling users

Enabling and disabling users is similar to deleting users. Select the users you want to enable/disable from the **User Management** list, select **Enable** or **Disable** from the **Choose an Action** drop-down list and press **go**. The system will ask for confirmation before processing the request.

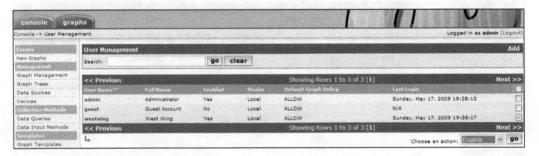

Copying users

If you have created a user who has a very complicated set of realm, graph, device, or template permissions and you want a new user to have the same permissions but do not want to go through the process of setting up all those permissions again, you can use the **Copy User** action. Select the user whose permissions you want to copy from the **User Management** list, then select **Copy** from the **Choose an Action** drop-down list and press **go**. You will get the following dialog box:

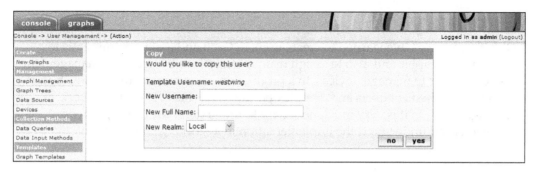

Fill in the **New Username**, **New Full Name** (optional), select the **New Realm** and press **yes**. A new user will be created based on the selected user. This new user will have the same permissions as the previous user. If an existing username is being used, the Cacti system will show an error message.

Batch copying

Let's explain batch copying with an example. There is a user called **westwing** who has access to view and edit several graphs in the Cacti system. Now, the administrator wants to give the same permission to **UserB** and **UserC** who are already in the system. Select **UserB** and **UserC**, from the **User Management** list and select **Batch Copy** from the **Choose an Action** drop-down list, and press **go**. The Cacti system will show the following dialog box. Now, the administrator has to select **Template User** from the list, in this example **westwing** is the **Template User**, and confirm the process by pressing **yes**.

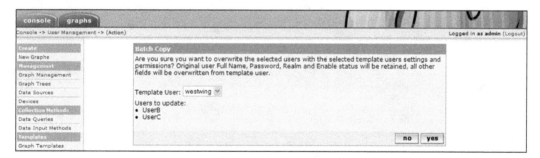

For further understanding, please consult the Cacti Manual or post your query in the Cacti forum.

[The official Cacti forum for technical support is `forums.cacti.net`.]

Summary

In this chapter, we have learned to create users in Cacti and assign permissions to view and edit graphs, and also to assign realm permissions to access the management console in order to manage devices. In a production environment, the administrator deals with hundreds of users and complex permission issues. It is tedious work to manage users, so it is very much necessary to understand the different types of permissions and understand the implementation in a working environment.

6
NET-SNMP

We have read about Cacti in the first chapter—Cacti is a complete web-based front-end for RRDTool. It has built-in SNMP capabilities, capable of polling data from SNMP-enabled network-attached devices, and processing selected data to produce graph using the RRDTool engine. So, we must have a working knowledge on SNMP (Simple Network Management Protocol), otherwise it will be hard to implement and manage Cacti. In this chapter, we will understand the basic data structure of SNMP, its process, command line tools, MIB definition, and then, we will look into NET-SNMP—an application suite for SNMP and its implementation in Cacti-network monitoring tool.

What is SNMP?

SNMP stands for Simple Network Management Protocol. It is a component of the Internet Protocol Suite commonly known as TCP/IP, defined by Internet Engineering Task Force (IETF). Developed in 1988 to provide network-device-monitoring capability for TCP/IP-based networks, SNMP was approved as an internet standard in 1990 by the Internet Architecture Board (IAB) and has been in wide use since that time. More recently, Internetwork Packet Exchange (IPX)-based networks have added support for SNMP. Currently, most network equipment vendors provide SNMP support in their products.

In a typical SNMP usage, there are number of systems or devices to manage, and one or more systems managing them. A software component called an agent runs on every managed system or devices and sends information back to the managing system through SNMP. SNMP agents expose management data on managed systems or devices—typically: memory, configuration, process, route and many more. Protocol also allows active management tasks such as applying or modifying configuration.

Variables accessed in different systems managed by SNMP, are organized in a hierarchical order. These hierarchies are described by MIBs (Management Information Bases). So, SNMP itself does not define which information a managed system should offer, rather it uses the extensive design offered by MIBs.

SNMP is part of the internet network management architecture. Network management model is comprised of several elements defined in different RFCs:

 In order to know more details about SNMP, see the following RFC: `http://www.ietf.org/rfc/rfc1157.txt`.

- Network elements—These are mostly network-attached, IP-enabled hardware such as a computer, router, switch, UPS, printer, and so on.

- Agents—Agents are software modules residing in network elements that are responsible for collecting and storing information such as errors, status, temperature, and configuration.

- Managed object—Managed object is a characteristic of a managed-system that can be managed.

- Management Information Base (MIB)—A MIB is a collection of managed objects stored in a virtual information database.

- Syntax notation—This is a language to describe MIB's managed objects in a machine independent format.

- Structure of Management Information (SMI)—SMI defines the rules for describing management information using ASN.1 (Abstract Syntax Notation). In order to learn more about ASN.1 visit http://www.itu.int/ITU-T/asn1/.

- Network Management Stations (NMSs)—These devices are used (such as a computer console) to execute management applications to monitor or configure network elements.

- Management Protocol—This is the protocol to interchange information between a managed system (network elements) and a managing system (NMSs). SNMP is the de facto standard management protocol.

How SNMP works?

Large networks with hundreds or thousands of nodes are difficult to manage without a large number of staff to monitor every computer. SNMP, which is widely used in local area networks (LANs), lets you monitor network nodes from a management host. You can monitor network devices such as servers, workstations, printers, routers, bridges, and hubs, as well as services such as Dynamic Host

Configuration Protocol (DHCP) or Windows Internet Name Service (WINS). So, the basic structure of SNMP consists of three main components:

1. Managed System (Network elements).
2. Agent (Network-management software).
3. Network-management stations (NMSs).

Managed System is a device or a node—such as (but not limited to) routers, switches, printers, servers, IPS, UPS in a managed network, which contains a built-in agent that collects and stores device-specific information, and also, makes the information available to NMSs through the SNMP protocol.

Agent is a software module built-in locally in a managed system, responsible for collecting and storing information; later this translates to an SNMP compatible form as per request from NMSs so that SNMP protocol can carry the information to NMSs.

SNMP applications run in a network management station (NMS) and issue queries to gather information about the status, configuration, and performance of external network devices called network elements. Shown below is a basic diagram illustrating the concept.

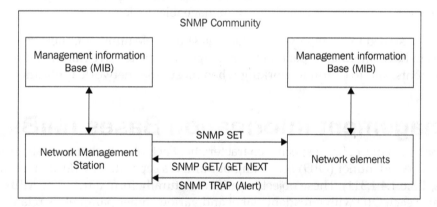

SNMP agents run in managed-systems (for example, in the Cisco 4500 router) and respond to NMS queries (GETs) (for example, from Cacti). In addition, agents send unsolicited reports (called traps) back to the NMS when certain network activity occurs. These traps can spawn events such as email alerts, automatic pages, or network server parameter modifications.

For security reasons, the SNMP agent validates each request from an SNMP manager before responding to the request, by verifying that the manager belongs to an SNMP community with access privileges to the agent.

An SNMP community is a logical relationship between an SNMP agent and one or more SNMP managers. The community has a name, and all the members of a community have the same access privileges: either read-only (members can view configuration and performance information) or read-write (members can view configuration and performance information, and also change the configuration if desired).

All SNMP message exchanges consist of a community name and a data field, which contains the SNMP operation and its associated operands. It is embedded within a UDP Datagram, inside an IP Packet within an Ethernet frame.

You can configure the SNMP agent to receive requests and send responses only from managers that are members of a known community. If the agent knows the community name in the SNMP message, and knows that the manager generating the request is a member of that community, it considers the message to be authentic and gives it the access allowed for members of that community. Thus, the SNMP community prevents unauthorized managers from viewing or changing the configuration of a router or other SNMP manageable device.

SNMP is designed to be deployed on the largest possible number of network devices, to have minimal impact on the managed nodes, to have minimal transport requirements, and to continue working when most other network applications fail.

Management Information Bases (MIBs)

Each managed object has a specific characteristic. Each object/characteristic has a unique object identifier (OID) consisting of numbers separated by decimal points (that is, 1.3.6.1.4.1.311). These object identifiers naturally form a tree. The MIB associates each OID with a readable label and various other parameters related to the object. The MIB then serves as a data dictionary or code book that is used to assemble and interpret SNMP messages.

When an SNMP manager wants to know the value of an object/characteristic, such as the state of an alarm point, the system name, or the element uptime, it will assemble a GET packet that includes the OID for each object/characteristic of interest. The network element receives the request and looks up each OID in its code book (MIB), if the OID is found (the object is managed by the network element), a response packet is assembled and sent with the current value of the object/characteristic included. If the OID is not found, a special error response is sent that identifies the unmanaged object.

SNMP additionally allows the extension of these standard values with values specific to a particular agent through the use of private MIBs.

Directives, issued by the network manager client to an SNMP agent, consist of the identifiers of SNMP variables (referred to as MIB object identifiers (OID) or MIB variables) along with instructions to either get the value for the identifier, or set the identifier to a new value.

Through the use of private MIB variables (OIDs), SNMP agents can be tailored for a myriad of specific devices, such as network bridges, gateways, and routers. The definitions of MIB variables supported by a particular agent are incorporated in descriptor files, written in Abstract Syntax Notation (ASN.1) format, made available to network management client programs, so that they can become aware of these MIB variables and their usage.

The IETF grants authority for parts of the name space to individual organizations such as Microsoft, Novell, or CIsco. For example, Microsoft has the authority to assign the OIDs that can be derived by branching downward from the node in the MIB name tree that starts with 1.3.6.1.4.1.311. Novell's OIDs branch down from 1.3.6.1.4.1.23. and Cisco's OIDs branch down from 1.3.6.1.4.1.9. You can see this structure in the following diagram.

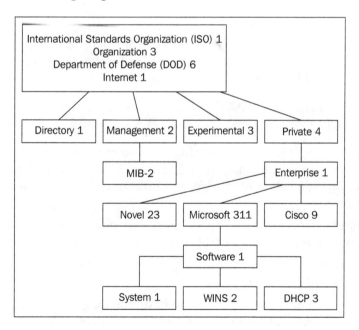

SNMP uses the OID to identify objects on each network element (that is router/ computer) that can be managed using SNMP. For example, in order to get information about the free disk space on a Windows NT Server, the Network Management Station makes a request to the network element using the fully qualified OID that represents the variable containing the number representing the free disk space. In Microsoft's world, that would be .1.3.6.1.4.1.311.1.1.3.1.1.5.1.4.0. or something very similar, depending how the MIB for that object was created. A Cisco 4500 router's CPU usage is accessed by targeting the OID .1.3.6.1.4.1.9.2.1.56.0. For a list of object identifier, check the URL `http://www.iana.org/assignments/ enterprise-numbers`.

Comparison of SNMP versions and security

Currently, there are three versions of SNMP: SNMP v1, SNMP v2, and SNMP v3. Version 1 and 2 have a number of features in common, but SNMP v2 offers enhancements—such as additional protocol and 64-bit high capacity counter for high-speed interface. SNMP v3 adds security and remote configuration capabilities to the previous versions.

SNMP v1 works over protocols such as UDP, IP, OSI Connectionless Network Service (CLNS), AppleTalk Datagram-Delivery Protocol (DDP), and Novell Internet Packet Exchange (IPX). SNMP v1 is widely used and is the de facto network management protocol in the internet community.

Request/response behavior of SNMP is implemented by using four protocol operations—Get, GetNext, Set, and Trap.

- 'Get' operation is used by managing the system to retrieve the value of one or more instance from an agent. If the agent responding to the Get operation cannot provide values of all objectfg fd instances in a list, it does not provide any values.
- 'GetNext' operation is used by the managing system to collect the value of the next object instance in a table or a list within an agent.
- 'Set' operation is used by the managing system to set values of object instances within an agent.
- 'Trap' operation is used by agents to inform managing system about significant events in network-attached SNMP-enabled devices.

SNMP v1 has some problems such as authentication of the message source, protecting message from disclosure, and placing access controls on the MIB database. SNMP v2 was designed back in 1993, and was an evolution of its predecessor. Get, GetNext, and Set operations remain the same in SNMP v2 but SNMP v2 adds and enhances some operations. In SNMP v2, when multiple requests are made by the 'get' request, if one request is not valid or does not exist, there will answers for the other requests, whereas in SNMP v1 no response at all was given, only the error message. SNMP v2 simplifies the traps operation by giving the same format as get and set operations.

SNMP v2 also defines two new protocol operations: 'GetBulk' and 'Inform'. GetBulk operation is used by the managing device to retrieve large blocks of data, such as multiple rows of table. The Inform operation allows managing devices to send trap information to another managing device and to then receive response.

A major change in SNMP v2 is improved security that was missing in SNMP v1. Later, SNMP v3 added additional security and remote administration capabilities. The SNMP v3 architecture introduced the user-based security model for message security and the view-based Access Control Model for access control. It also supports concurrent use of different security, access control, and message processing models. SNMP v3 has the ability to dynamically configure an SNMP agent using SNMP Set command against MIB object that represent the agent's configuration.

Security is important when using SNMP, as an example, its ability to reboot managed devices; the administrator cannot let this ability be violated. SNMP v1 used only one type of security — community names. Agents can be set to reply to queries only received by accepted community names. In SNMP v1, the community name was passed in data packet in clear text. This allowed hackers to capture the data packet and learn the SNMP community name and password. SNMP v2 brought a lot of extra security. Everything in the packet is encrypted except the destination address. Inside the encrypted data is the community name and source IP address. The agent decodes and uses the community name and accepted source IP to validate request. SNMP v3 provides the latest architecture for SNMP security. It incorporates an SNMP context engine ID to encode and decode SNMP contexts. It matches a context name with an object and the security requires the object and context to match. SNMP v3 provides three levels of security — highest level with authentication and privacy, middle level with authentication without privacy, and bottom level without authentication and privacy.

Net-SNMP

The Net-SNMP application suite implements SNMP v1, SNMP v2c, and SNMP v3 using IPv4 and IPv6. It has a command line application to retrieve information from SNMP-enabled network-attached devices, and also manipulate configuration, and convert between numerical and textual MIB OIDs. It has a graphical MIB browser, a daemon application that receives SNMP trap notification, and a set of libraries to develop new SNMP application using C and Perl APIs.

Cacti uses Net-SNMP application suite to retrieve raw data from SNMP-enabled devices, and then uses the RRDTool to create graphics using raw data. In order to run Cacti the managing system needs to run Net-SNMP. If you need to install Net-SNMP manually, please see the Net-SNMP manual page: `http://www.net-snmp.org/docs/man/`.

These days, we don't need to install Net-SNMP manually in the managing system. There are distribution specific tools to install the application, such as **yum** in Fedora core, **apt-get** in Ubuntu. After installation, run following command to ensure Net-SNMP is running.

```
snmpwalk -v 2c -c public localhost system
```

This should return an output like following:

```
SNMPv2-MIB::sysDescr.0 = STRING: Linux ubuntu01 2.6.24-20-generic
#1 SMP Mon Jul 28 13:49:52 UTC 2008 i686
SNMPv2-MIB::sysObjectID.0 = OID: NET-SNMP-MIB::netSnmpAgentOIDs.10
DISMAN-EVENT-MIB::sysUpTimeInstance = Timeticks: (175589)
0:29:15.89
SNMPv2-MIB::sysContact.0 = STRING: Root   (configure /etc/snmp/
snmpd.local.conf)
SNMPv2-MIB::sysName.0 = STRING: ubuntu01
SNMPv2-MIB::sysLocation.0 = STRING: Unknown (configure /etc/snmp/
snmpd.local.conf)
SNMPv2-MIB::sysORLastChange.0 = Timeticks: (0) 0:00:00.00
SNMPv2-MIB::sysORID.1 = OID: SNMP-FRAMEWORK-MIB::
snmpFrameworkMIBCompliance
SNMPv2-MIB::sysORID.2 = OID: SNMP-MPD-MIB::snmpMPDCompliance
SNMPv2-MIB::sysORID.3 = OID: SNMP-USER-BASED-SM-MIB::
usmMIBCompliance
SNMPv2-MIB::sysORID.4 = OID: SNMPv2-MIB::snmpMIB
SNMPv2-MIB::sysORID.5 = OID: TCP-MIB::tcpMIB
SNMPv2-MIB::sysORID.6 = OID: IP-MIB::ip
SNMPv2-MIB::sysORID.7 = OID: UDP-MIB::udpMIB
SNMPv2-MIB::sysORID.8 = OID: SNMP-VIEW-BASED-ACM-MIB::
```

```
vacmBasicGroup
SNMPv2-MIB::sysORDescr.1 = STRING: The SNMP Management
Architecture MIB.
SNMPv2-MIB::sysORDescr.2 = STRING: The MIB for Message Processing
and Dispatching.
SNMPv2-MIB::sysORDescr.3 = STRING: The management information
definitions for the SNMP User-based Security Model.
SNMPv2-MIB::sysORDescr.4 = STRING: The MIB module for SNMPv2
entities
SNMPv2-MIB::sysORDescr.5 = STRING: The MIB module for managing TCP
implementations
SNMPv2-MIB::sysORDescr.6 = STRING: The MIB module for managing IP
and ICMP implementations
SNMPv2-MIB::sysORDescr.7 = STRING: The MIB module for managing UDP
implementations
SNMPv2-MIB::sysORDescr.8 = STRING: View-based Access Control Model
for SNMP.
```

Cacti also runs in the Windows operating system. But it is beyond the scope of this book. There is a chapter in the Cacti manual that is a step-by-step guide to install SNMP tool, RRDTool, WAMP (Windows, Apache, MySQL, PHP) and Cacti: `http://www.cacti.net/downloads/docs/html/install_windows.html`.

Basic Net-SNMP commands

In Cacti, we do not need to work with Net-SNMP command line applications on a day-to-day basis. But we need to have knowledge on basic Net-SNMP command line tools to troubleshoot. If you are new to Net-SNMP, then a good place to start is the tutorial section: `http://www.net-snmp.org/wiki/index.php/Tutorials`.

According to the Net-SNMP manual, it is divided in different sections, such as SNMP basic applications, SNMP "second-level" applications, notifications, SNMP configuration, agent, SNMP base library APIs, agent APIs. We will not discuss details of each command; you can get the details in the manual page: `http://www.net-snmp.org/docs/man/`.

Summary

In this chapter, we saw how Simple Network Management Protocol works—its process to work with network-attached SNMP-enabled devices. We also saw how Net-SNMP application suite implements SNMP and Cacti uses Net-SNMP to retrieve raw data from managed-system, and then use RRDTool to create graphs for easy understanding.

7
Data Management

To generate graphs, Cacti needs to collect data. Cacti, by default, comes with some data queries and data input methods, which are enough for small and medium networks, but if you have a large network with 100+ computers, routers, and network devices, writing some data queries and input methods may save you time.

In this chapter, we will learn:

- How to create data input method.
- How to create data query.
- SNMP query XML syntax.
- Script query XML syntax.
- Creating graph for single SNMP OID.

In Cacti, data is collected by two methods:

1. The data input method.
2. The data query method.

Data input method

In Chapter 4, we learned about the data input method. Here, we'll learn to create data input methods. Data input methods are the basic system that Cacti uses to collect data for generating graphs.

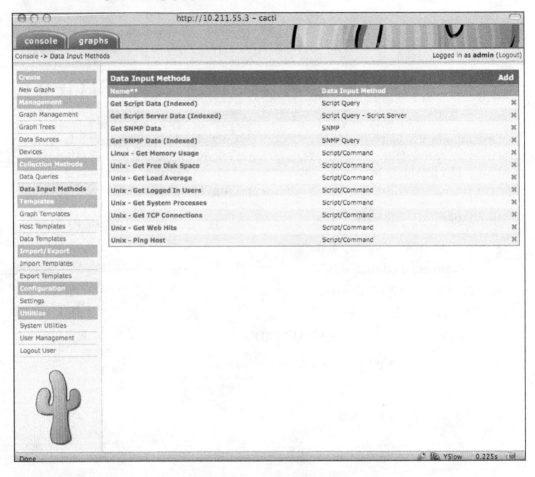

In the above figure, we can see the list of input methods that come with Cacti. For most small networks, you don't need to add or create a custom data input method. For larger networks, writing your own data input method may help you as then, you have more control over your graph.

For example, a web server administrator might want to know how many Apache child processes are running. With Cacti, you can show the number of processes on a device without adding any new data input methods. However, if we want to count the instances of a particular process, one option is to create a new data input method. In the following example, we will assume that the process is on the local Cacti box.

To do this, we will use a Perl script. First, create a file called `num_process.pl` in the Cacti `script` folder. Then, paste the following code in this file:

```
#!/usr/bin/perl
system "ps ax|grep $ARGV[0]|wc -l";
```

This script needs one input, and that is the process name that you want to count. Then, it will print the number of processes of the given type. To test the script, run `perl num_process.pl apache` in the terminal. This script will display the count of the number of processes of Apache. Now, we'll see how to create a data input method using this query.

Creating a data input method

To add a new data input method, click the **add** button in the top right corner. You will get another page, with some fields.

In the above figure, we can see three fields that we have to fill in. Below is the description of the fields:

Fields	Details
Name	Here, we need to fill in the name of the data input method. Giving a job-related name is the best practice.
Input type	This is basically how the data will be collected. The possible types are: **SNMP**, **SNMP query**, **Script/command**, **Script query**, **Script- Script Server** (PHP), and **Script query –Script server**.
Input string	This field is only for the input type **Script/Command**. Here, you have to enter the full address of the script and also the variable (if needed). Example: `perl <path_cacti>/scripts/ping.pl <ip>`. Here, `<path_cacti>` will be replaced with the current Cacti installation path on runtime. The rest is the address of the script. As this is a Perl script, you have to use `perl` at beginning of the line. `<ip>` is the input for the script, which is optional.

Let's fill in these fields with my example data:

Name: Number of Process.

Input Type: Script.

Input String: perl <path_cacti>/scripts/num_process.pl <processname>.

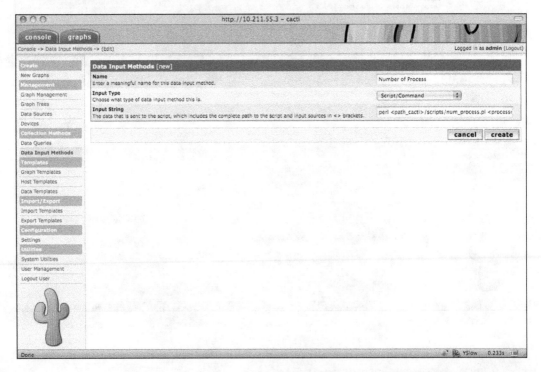

After filling in all the fields, click on the **create** button.

After the initial creation of the input method, you will be redirected back to this page. Now, you have to add input and output fields.

Input fields

Input fields are optional for data input method, so if you are not using any input, skip this section.

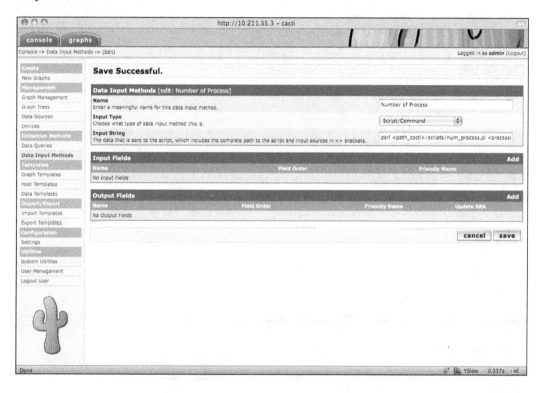

For our input string, we passed **<processname>** as the parameter to this script, now we have to add this as an input field. To add an input field, press on **Add** on the right side of **Input Field** section. Then, we will get another form, asking for some more fields.

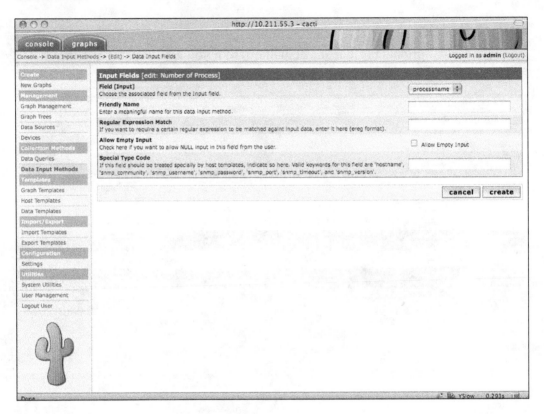

Fields details of this form are as follows:

Fields	Details
Field [Input]	Select the input from the drop down list. Here, you will get all the parameters that had given in the input string.
Friendly Name	Give a friendly name for this input field.
Regular Expression Match	If you want a certain regular expression to be matched against the input data, enter it here. The regular expression must follow POSIX syntax as it will be passed to PHP's ereg() function.

Fields	Details
Allow Empty Input	Check it, if you want to allow an empty input.
Special Type Code	Sometimes, Cacti needs to reference a field internally, but relying on more than just the field name. For instance, if your field requires an IP address from the user, you can enter 'management_ip' here and Cacti will fill this field in with the current IP address of the selected host. Valid values for this field are: 'hostname', 'management_ip', 'snmp_community', 'snmp_username', 'snmp_password', and 'snmp_version'.

In our example, we have an input called **processname**, so we have to add an input field. Let's fill in the input fields form:

Field [input]: Select **processname**.

Friendly Name: Name of the process.

Regular Expression Match: {blank} (as we don't need it, keep it empty).

Allow Empty Input: {Unselected} (we will not allow empty input, don't select it)

Special Type Code: {blank} (we don't need it, keep it empty).

Now, click **create**.

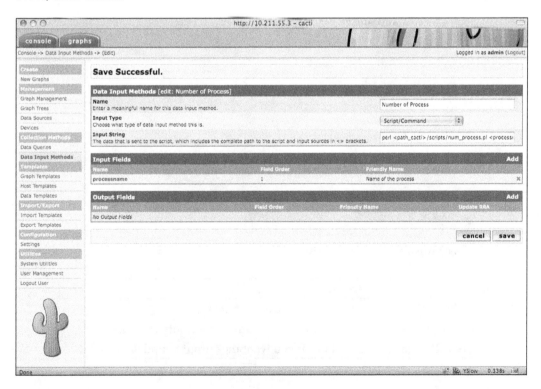

You will be redirected to the previous page, but now you will see a new row on the **Input Fields** section, like this screenshot. We have only one input, so we will now complete the output field. Do it again if you have more than one input field.

Output fields

Like the input field, to add an output field, click **Add** from the **Output fields** section. You will get another page with some fields.

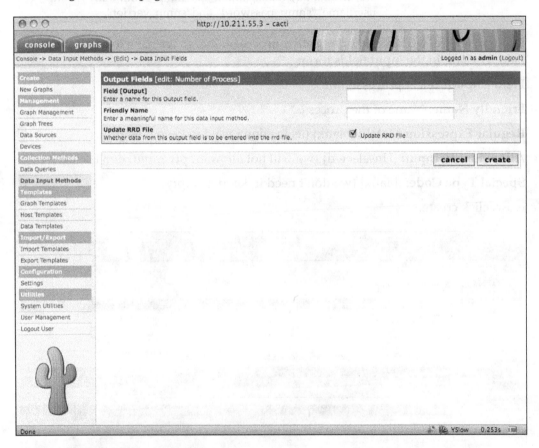

Field details of this form are as follows:

Fields	Details
Field [Output]	The name of the output field.
Friendly Name	Give a meaningful name for the output field.
Update RRD File	Select this if you want the output to update the RRD file.

Now, fill in these fields:

Field [Output]: numprocess.

Friendly Name: Number of Process.

Update RRD File: {Selected} (Check it).

After filling in the fields, click on the **create** button. You will be redirected to the previous page, with a new row in the **Output Fields** section.

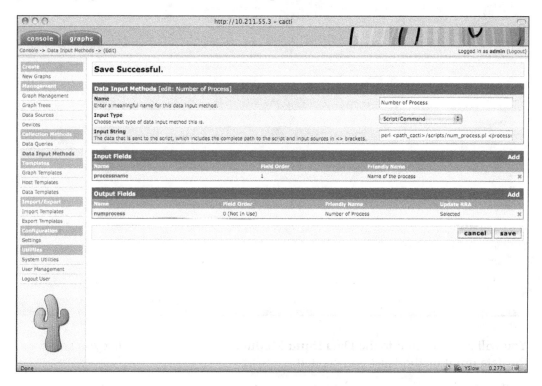

We are done. Click on **Save** to save the changes.

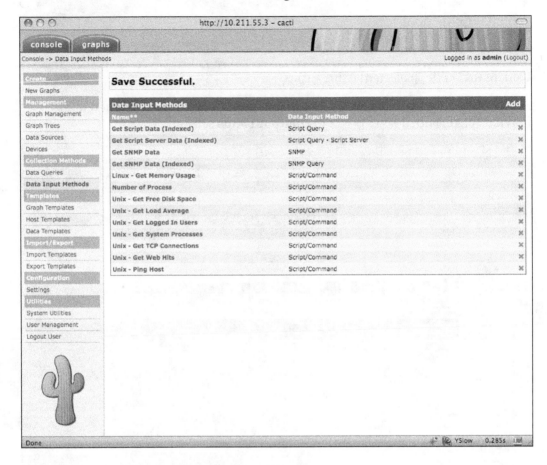

You will be redirected to the **Data Input Methods** page, and on the list you will see the data input method just you created.

We are done, now you can use this input method to create a data template.

Data queries

Data queries are not a replacement for data input methods in Cacti. Instead, they provide an easy way to query or list data based upon an index making the data easier to graph. The most common use of a data query within Cacti is to retrieve a list of network interfaces via SNMP. If you want to graph the traffic of a network interface, first Cacti must retrieve a list of interfaces on the host. Second, Cacti can use that information to create the necessary graphs and data sources. Data queries are only concerned with the first step of the process that is obtaining a list of network interfaces and not creating the graphs/data sources for them. While listing network interfaces is a common use for data queries, they also have other uses such as listing partitions, processors, or even cards in a router.

These are the default data queries that come with the Cacti default installation:

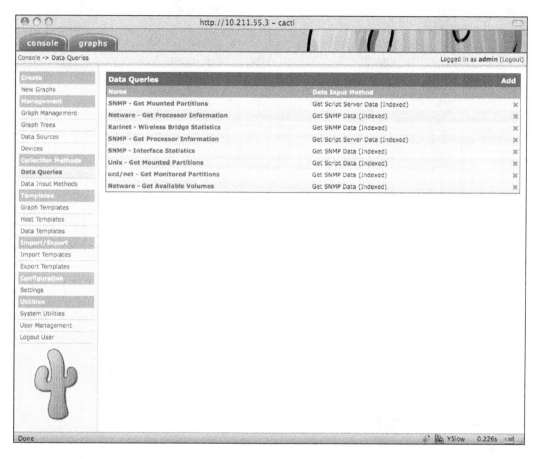

One requirement for any data query in Cacti is that it needs some unique value that defines each row in the list. This concept follows that of a 'primary key' in SQL, and makes sure that each row in the list can be uniquely referenced. Examples of these index values are 'ifIndex' for SNMP network interfaces or the device name for partitions. There are two types of data queries that you will see referred to throughout Cacti. They are script queries and SNMP queries. Script and SNMP queries are virtually identical in their functionality and only differ in how they obtain their information. A script query will call an external command or script and an SNMP query will make an SNMP call to retrieve a list of data.

Creating a data query

All data queries have two parts, the XML file and the definition within Cacti. An XML file must be created for each query. The XML file defines where each piece of information is and how to retrieve it. This could be thought of as the actual query. The second part is a definition within Cacti, which tells Cacti where to find the XML file and associates the data query with one or more graph templates. I will describe the XML syntax later on in this chapter. Before we create the XML file, we'll create the definition for the data query. Click on **Add**, you will get another page with some basic input field.

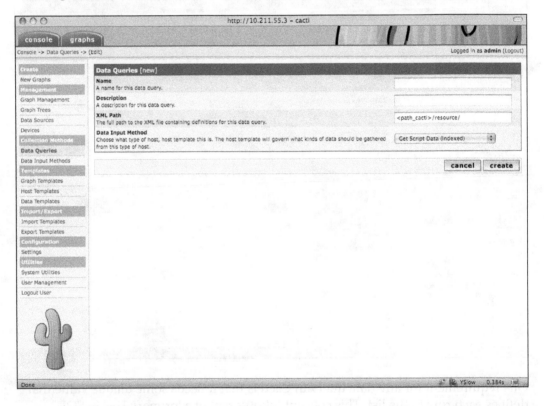

Field details of this form:

Fields	Details
Name	Give a name for your new data query here.
Description	Write a short message (what the query will do). Try to make it as meaningful as possible.

Fields	Details
XML Path	The most important part-write the full path of the XML file that you just created. You can use `<path_cacti>` variable, Cacti will substitute the actual path during execution, allowing for greater portability.
Data Input Method	Here, you have to tell how Cacti will store the retrieved data. Select **Get SNMP Data (indexed)** if you are using SNMP and **Get Script Data (indexed)** if you are using script query.

After filling all these fields press the **create** button. Cacti will check if the XML file is available on the given path, if not it will show the warning **Could not locate XML file**. The data queries will be created.

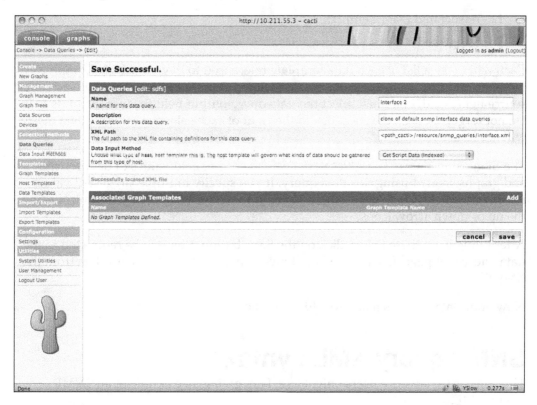

After successfully creating the data query, you will get this page. Every data query must have at least one graph template associated with it, and possibly more depending on the number of output fields specified in the XML file.

Associated Graph Templates

To add associated graph templates, click **Add** from Associated Graph Templates. You get another page with two fields of input. Field's details:

Fields	Details
Name	Give a name for this associated graph.
Graph Template	Select the graph template that you want to associate with this data query.

After filling in these fields, click on the **create** button. You will be redirected back to same page, but this time you will get two more sections on the page called:

1. **Associated Data Templates**.
2. **Suggested Values**.

Cacti will make a list of each data template referenced to in your selected graph template and display them under the **Associated Data Templates** box. For each data source item listed, you must select the data query output field that corresponds to it. Do not forget to check the checkbox to the right of each selection, or your data query will not be active.

The **Suggested Values** box gives you a way to control field values of data sources and graphs created using this data query. If you specify multiple suggested values for the same field, Cacti will evaluate them in the order which you can control using the up or down arrow icons.

After filling in all these fields, click on the **Save** button. You will be redirected to the data query edit page. Do this as many times as needed to add all your data from the XML file.

Now your data query is ready to add to any host.

SNMP query XML syntax

This topic is for advance users only. Here, I am giving an example of an SNMP Query XML.

```
<query>
    <name>Get SNMP Interfaces</name>
    <description>Queries a host for a list of monitorable interfaces</
description>
    <oid_uptime>.1.3.x.x.x</oid_uptime>
    <oid_index>.1.3.6.1.2.1.2.2.1.1</oid_index>
```

```
    <oid_index_parse>OID/REGEXP:.*\.([0-9]{1,3}\.[0-9]{1,3})$</oid_
index_parse>
    <oid_num_indexes>.1.3.6.1.2.1.2.1.0</oid_num_indexes>
    <index_order>ifDescr:ifName:ifIndex</index_order>
    <index_order_type>numeric</index_order_type>
    <index_title_format>|chosen_order_field|</index_title_format>
    <fields>
        <ifIndex>
            <name>Index</name>
            <method>walk</method>
            <source>value</source>
            <direction>input</direction>
            <oid>.1.3.6.1.2.1.2.2.1.1</oid>
        </ifIndex>
    </fields>
</query>
```

Here are the details of these fields:

Field	Details
query->name	Give a 'friendly name' for the SNMP query here. Cacti will not use it, and is for identification only. This field is optional.
query->description	Enter a description for the SNMP query here. Cacti will not use it, and it is for identification only. This field is optional.
query->oid_uptime	If you have another OID that contains timetics, then, you can create a data query that specifies an alternate Uptime OID. Then, if you select your re-index method to be Uptime Goes Backward, Cacti will use that OID to detect whether it is time to re-index the host instead of the standard SNMP OID for uptime.
query->oid_index	In any SNMP query, it must have an OID that represents the index values for the query when walked.
query->oid_index_parse	It is required only when you are trying to parse the unique index from the OID itself. If this field is defined, to obtain a list of indexes, Cacti walks the OID provided in the oid_index field above. It then applies the regular expression provided in this field to the list of OIDs that are returned. The matched substrings that remain become the list of indexes for this SNMP query.

Field	Details
query->oid_num_indexes	This OID is used to determine the total number of available index. If specified, this will be used to determine when to automatically re-cache this SNMP query when it is attached to a device.
query->index_order	Generally, Cacti will try to find the best field to index off based on whether each row in the query is unique and non-null. If you give it, Cacti will perform this check on the fields listed here in the order you specify. Here, only input fields are allowed and if you need multiple fields, use colon as separator.
query->index_order_type	Here, you need to define the type of sorting for the index. The type of the sorting can be one of these two types:
	Numeric: The indexes in this SNMP query are to be sorted numerically (that is,1,2,3,10,20,31).
	Alphabetic: The indexes in this SNMP query are to be sorted alphabetically (that is,1,10,2,20,3,31).
query->index_title_format	Enter the title format to use when representing an index to the user. Here you can use any input field name as a variable by enclosing it in pipes (|).
query->fields	Here, you need to define all the fields that are used in the SNMP query.
query->fields->ifIndex	Give an unique name to all the defined fields in the SNMP query. Space and non-alphanumeric characters are not allowed here. (and it's required to be identifiable).
query->fields->ifIndex->name	Specify a 'friendly name' for the field. Cacti will use this to help the user identify this field.
query->fields->ifIndex->method	Here, you can specify which method it will use to collect SNMP information for this field. The possible methods are get and walk. Though walk is more efficient then get, both of them will return the same value.
	Get: The get method obtains a list of indexes and does an snmpget for each index of the OID specified for this field.
	Walk: The walk method does a walk of the OID specified for this field.

Field	Details
query->fields->ifIndex->source	For every field you need to tell Cacti how to derive its values for each row. The possible values are: `value`, `OID/REGEXP`, `VALUE/REGEXP`, and `index`.
	`Value`: The 'value' option simply returns the result of the snmpget for each row.
	`OID/REGEXP:(regexp_match)`: This can be used when you need to use a POSIX-based regular expression to derive the value from the OID.
	`VALUE/REGEXP:(regexp_match)`: This option can be used to parse the value based on a regular expression, returning the first match.
	`index`: Simply use the value of the index for this row as the value. If the index is being parsed from the OID using the `oid_index_parse` field, you must specify `index` here.
query->fields->ifIndex->direction	Here the possible values are input and output.
	Input: Input values are the 'known' values that you will use to derive the output values; this is where the 'query' part of SNMP query comes in. When you create a graph based on an SNMP query, Cacti will prompt you to choose the input value to base the graph on.
	Output: Output values are 'unknown' values that are returned from the script. An SNMP query may return multiple statistics for a single index. For instance, a single interface could return bytes/sec in, errors, packets/sec, and so on.
	A rule of thumb is that input fields contain semi-static data that is not graphable, while the output fields contain the data that will be graphed.
query->fields->ifIndex-> oid	This field is required. Specify the actual OID that corresponds with the field. Each value for this field can be obtained by doing an `snmpget` on `oid.(each)snmpindex`.

Script Query XML

If you need to write Script query XML, here is the syntax:

```
<query>
    <name>Get Unix Mounted Partitions</name>
    <description>Queries a list of mounted partitions on a unix-based
host with the 'df' command.</description>
```

```
<script_path>perl |path_cacti|/scripts/query_unix_partitions.pl
        </script_path>
 <arg_index>index</arg_index>
<arg_query>query</arg_query>
<arg_get>get</arg_get>
<arg_num_indexes>num_indexes</arg_num_indexes>
<output_delimeter>:</output_delimeter>
<index_order>dskDevice:dskMount</index_order>
 <index_order_type>alphabetic</index_order_type>
<index_title_format>|chosen_order_field|</index_title_format>
<fields>
    <dskDevice>
        <name>Device Name</name>
        <direction>input</direction>
        <query_name>device</query_name>
    </dskDevice>
</fields>
</query>
```

And here is the detail of the XML tags.

Fields	Details
query->name	Give a 'friendly name' for the SNMP query here. Cacti will not use it, and is for identification only. This field is optional.
query->description	Enter a description for the SNMP query here. Cacti will not use it, and is for identification only. This field is optional.
query->script_path	Here, you need to give the complete path of the script. When in doubt, specify the pull path to all binaries referenced in this path, the query may not execute otherwise.
query->arg_index	This is the argument that is to be passed to the script to retrieve a list of indexes.
query->arg_query	The argument that is to be passed to the script to retrieve a list of values given a field name.
query->arg_get	Enter the argument that is to be passed to the script to retrieve a single value given a field name and index value.
query->arg_num_indexes	Enter the argument that is to be passed to the script to determine the total number of available indexes. If specified, this will be used to determine when to automatically re-cache this script query when it is attached to a device.
query->output_delimeter	Enter the one character delimiter that will be used to separate output values. This is only used when you 'query' the script in which case it outputs 'index(delimiter)value'.

Fields	Details
query->index_ order	Cacti will attempt to find the best field to index off of based on whether each row in the query is unique and non-null. If specified, Cacti will perform this check on the fields listed here in the order specified. Only input fields can be specified and multiple fields should be delimited with a comma.
query->index_ order_type	Here, you need to define the type of sorting for the index. The type of the sorting can be one of these two types: Numeric: The indexes in this script query are to be sorted numerically (that is, 1,2,3,10,20,31). Alphabetic: The indexes in this script query are to be sorted alphabetically (that is, 1,10,2,20,3,31).
query->index_ title_format	Specify the title format to use when representing an index to the user. Any input field name can be used as a variable if enclosed in pipes (|). The variable |chosen_order_field| will be substituted with the field chosen by Cacti to index off of (see index_order above).
query->fields	Each field contained within the script query must be defined under this tag.
query->fields- >dskDevice	Each defined field in the script query must have a unique name given to it. Do not use spaces or any non-alphanumeric characters, this name must be identifiable within Cacti.
query->fields- >dskDevice- >name	Here, you can specify a 'friendly name' for the field. This name will be used by Cacti to help the user identify this field.
query->fields- >dskDevice- >direction	Input: Input values are the 'known' values that you will use to derive the output values; this is where the 'query' part of script query comes in. When you create a graph based on a script query, Cacti will prompt you to choose the input value to base the graph on. Output: Output values are 'unknown' values that are returned from the script. A script query may return multiple statistics for a single index. For instance, a single partition could return free disk space, total disk space, fragmentation percentage, and so on. A rule of thumb is that input fields contain semi-static data that is not graphable, while the output fields contain the data that will be graphed.
query->fields- >dskDevice- >query_name	Enter the name that Cacti must use when asking the script for information about this field. For instance, the following should return values: '(script_name) query (query_name)'.

Creating a graph for single SNMP OID

At some point, you may want to generate a graph for a single SNMP OID. In this section, we will learn to create a graph for SNMP OID.

To create a graph for SNMP OID we will use the **SNMP – Generic OID Template** that comes with all Cacti version 0.8.5 and above. Let's start!

Click **New Graph** from the **Create** section.

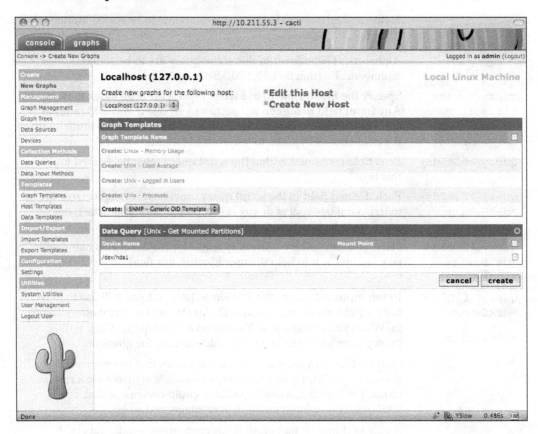

Now, from dropdown menu, select the host where you want to create the graph. From the next dropdown menu, select **SNMP – Generic OID Template** and click on the **create** button.

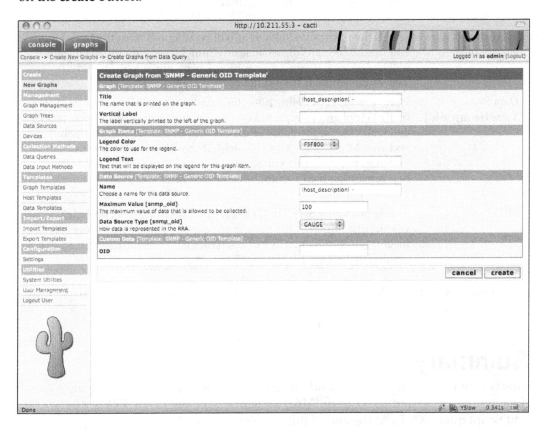

In the following page, you will need to fill in the fields.

Fields details of this form:

Field	Details
Title	Give the title for the new graph. Give a meaningful name, so that you can identify this graph later. It is always good idea to keep |host_description| as it is, just add your desired title after this.
Vertical Label	This will be printed on the graph left side (y-axis). It's generally used to describe units, such as 'bytes' or 'percent'.
Legend Color	The color that will be used to represent the data on the graph.
Legend Text	It will be used to describe the data on the graph legend.

Field	Details
Name	Enter the title of the data source. It is a good idea to keep |host_description| in the title, it will make the data source easier to identify later.
Maximum Value [snmp_oid]	This is the maximum value that will be accepted from the OID. Here, you need to be careful, because anything larger than the maximum will be ignored. If you are graphing a percentage, you should use '100' as the value. It should never exceed this.
Data Source Type [snmp_oid]	Here, you need to define how the data from the OID should be stored by RRDTool and interpreted on the graph. Possible values are GAUGE and COUNTER. If the value of the OID represents the actual data, you should use GAUGE for this field. If the OID value is a constantly incrementing number, you should use COUNTER for this field. The two remaining field values, DERIVE and ABSOLUTE can be ignored in most situations.
OID	This is the actual SNMP OID to graph. It is typically a good idea to enter the number OID here as opposed to using MIB names. For instance, to get the number of open files on a Netware server, so you would use '.1.3.6.1.4.1.23.2.28.2.7.0' as the OID.

After filling in all these fields, click on the **create** button. You are done. You can now manage this new graph from graph management.

Summary

This is very important chapter for advanced users. Here, we learned to create a new data input method and data query. Also, we learned the details of SNMP query XML and Script query XML. At the end of this chapter, we saw how to create a graph for a single SNMP OID.

8
Cacti Management

In this chapter, we are going to learn some advanced topics like:

- Cacti's directory structure.
- Cacti's backup procedure.
- Cacti's restore procedure.
- Cacti's CLI features.

Although Cacti is primarily a web-based PHP application, there are several command line interface scripts that allow for command line control of various aspects of Cacti. At the end of this chapter, we will cover some of these utilities.

Directory structure

Cacti's directory structure looks like the following:

```
lavlu@test-server-rnd: ~/src/cacti
File  Edit  View  Terminal  Tabs  Help
lavlu@test-server-rnd:~/src/cacti$ ls
about.php                    graphs_items.php              poller_commands.php
auth_changepassword.php      graphs_new.php                poller_export.php
auth_login.php               graphs.php                    poller.php
cacti.sql                    graph_templates_inputs.php    README
cdef.php                     graph_templates_items.php     resource
cli                          graph_templates.php           rra
cmd.php                      graph_view.php                rra.php
color.php                    graph_xport.php               scripts
config.php                   host.php                      script_server.php
data_input.php               host_templates.php            script_server.pl
data_queries.php             images                        settings.php
data_sources.php             include                       templates_export.php
data_templates.php           index.php                     templates_import.php
docs                         install                       tree.php
gprint_presets.php           lib                           user_admin.php
graph_image.php              LICENSE                       utilities.php
graph.php                    log
graph_settings.php           logout.php
lavlu@test-server-rnd:~/src/cacti$
```

Cacti contains the following sub-directories within its main directory — unless you are fully aware of the implications of editing these files, it is best to avoid doing so.

1. `cli` — This directory contains the Command Line Interface scripts that allow for console control over various aspects of Cacti. This can be likened to a `bin` directory.

2. `docs` — The Cacti manual and help documents are available here.

3. `images` — These are the images required by the Cacti GUI.

4. `include` — Cacti's main configuration and global files.

5. `install` — The installation directory. This folder will be used only at the time of installing Cacti, so it's always a good practice to remove this folder after successfully installing Cacti.

6. `lib` — The library directory — these files contain the majority of Cacti function calls.

7. `log` — Cacti stores all its log files in this directory. When debugging Cacti, this folder is very important. Make sure that this folder is writable by the Cacti user.

8. `resources` — This folder has three more sub-folders:
    ◦ `script_queries` — It holds the XML data queries.
    ◦ `script_server` — It holds the PHP or Perl queries.
    ◦ `snmp_queries` — It holds the SNMP query definitions in XML format.

9. `rra` — This is the most important folder for Cacti, because it holds the `rrd` files that are generated by the RRDTool. This means all the collected data are stored here. You need to make sure this folder is writable by the Cacti user.

10. `scripts` — General scripts. These scripts can be written in any language supported by the platform.

So, these are the folders. You need to ensure that the `log/` and `rra/` folders are writeable by the Cacti user, and the other folders are read-only for the Web and the Cacti user.

Backup

A backup process is important for any software package. Let's say you have been running a Cacti server for one year. One day, you come into the office and find that your server hard drive has crashed. Now, you need to reinstall everything. Not only that, you have also lost all your old data. To save you from such a scenario, backup is your friend. I always recommend taking a full backup before upgrading. The Cacti backup process has two parts:

- File backup.
- Database backup.

File backup

At the beginning of this chapter, you got the list of Cacti folders. It is always best practice to make a complete backup of the folder:

```
$ cp -a /path/to/cacti/ /path/to/backup/cacti
```

Here, we used `cp` with the `a` switch. This is the same as `dpR`, which preserves link, mode, ownership, and timestamps and does it recursively. Or if you want to only keep a backup of very important files, just take a backup of the `rra`, `resources`, and `scripts` folder.

Database backup

Cacti supports MySQL as a database server. We will take a backup of the MySQL data using `mysqldump` that comes with the MySQL client. To know more about `mysqldump`, check `man mysqldump` in a console.

```
mysqldump -u{username} -p{password} cacti > cacti_xx_yy_zz.sql
```

Replace {username} and {password} with the username and password you used during the installation in Chapter 2. Replace xx_yy_zz with the date on which you are taking a backup. Now, save the dump file in a safe place.

Restoring from a backup

Now, it is time to restore your Cacti from the backup. Like the backup, the restore process also has two parts, first files and then the database. Before restoring it, we need to remove the old Cacti files:

```
$ rm -rf /path/to/oldcacti
```

This command will remove old Cacti files, so be careful before doing this. Then, we will restore files:

```
$ cp -a /path/to/backup/cacti /path/to/cacti
```

Your files are ready. Now, let's restore the database:

```
$ mysql -ucacti -pcacti987 cacti < cacti_xx_yy_zz.sql
```

This command will restore the database. You need to make sure that the MySQL server has a Cacti user with the appropriate password and also a blank database called `cacti`.

Our files and database are ready, now we have to create a cron job that will run `poller.php` every five minutes:

```
$ nano /etc/cron.d/cacti
```

And paste following text there:

```
*/5 * * * * www-data php /var/www/cacti/poller.php > /dev/null 2>&1
```

Now, open Cacti in your browser. If you are getting any MySQL related error, check that `includes/config.php` have the correct configuration for MySQL.

Poller cache

The poller cache holds all the commands that Cacti will issue during the polling process in an internal format. To view this cache, open Cacti, and visit **System Utilities**.

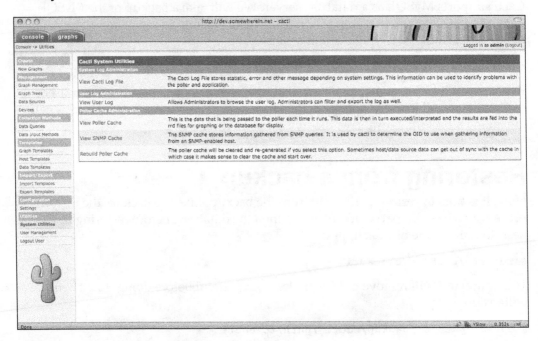

Now, click on **View Poller cache**. From this page, you can also view the Cacti log, user log, SNMP cache, and rebuild the poller cache.

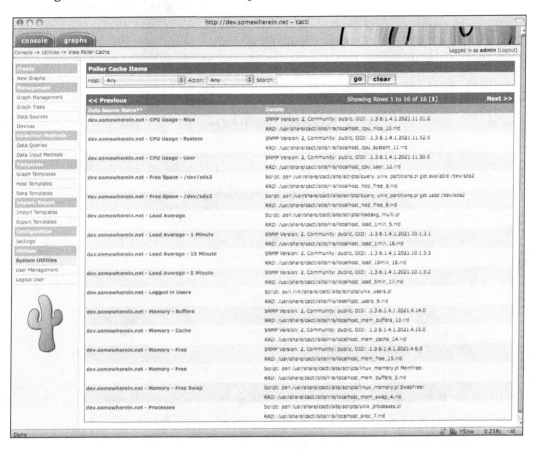

In this, you will get the list of poller cache. If you make any change to Cacti and the graphs stop updating, you need to rebuild the poller cache. To rebuild the poller cache, go to the previous page and click **Rebuild Poller cache**. If everything goes fine, you will get the same page shown in the above screenshot. Otherwise, it will show you an error.

Command Line Interface

Though Cacti's frontend is web-based, you can still do some task like rebuild poller cache, add new devices, add graphs, and so on, from the console. Here, I am showing you some basic syntax to maintain Cacti from command line. If you are not an advanced user, just skip this section. To see all the available command line PHP scripts, open the terminal and give this command:

```
$ ls /path/to/cacti/cli
```

You will get some PHP scripts. Some of them are described below:

1. `add_device.php`: This script is to add a device.
2. `add_graphs.php`: This script is to add graphs.
3. `add_perms.php`: This script is to add permissions to tree items.
4. `add_tree.php`: This script is to add objects to a tree.
5. `copy_user.php`: This is a Cacti user copy utility. It is highly recommended that you use the web interface to copy users as this script will only copy local Cacti users.
6. `poller_graphs_reapply_names.php`: This script is to rename a existing graph.
7. `poller_reindex_hosts.php`: This script is used to reindex all the data quires of a particular host.
8. `rebuild_poller_cache.php`: This script is to rebuild the poller cache.

As these are PHP scripts, you can run this through php cli. For better understanding, here is an example of rebuilding the poller cache from cli:

```
$ cd /path/to/cacti/cli
$ php   rebuild_poller_cache.php
```

The above command will clear the poller cache.

You can see the help for all these scripts at:

```
$ php   script_name.php -help
```

Summary

In this chapter, we first learned the folder structure of Cacti with their description. Here, we also learned how to back up and restore Cacti, which is very much important for any system admin. Cacti command line tools are very helpful for debugging and making a system administrator's job easy. But it's very much risky, so only an advance user should use these scripts.

Index

PACKT PUBLISHING

Thank you for buying
Cacti 0.8 Network Monitoring

Packt Open Source Project Royalties

When we sell a book written on an Open Source project, we pay a royalty directly to that project. Therefore by purchasing Cacti 0.8 Network Monitoring, Packt will have given some of the money received to the Cacti project.

In the long term, we see ourselves and you—customers and readers of our books—as part of the Open Source ecosystem, providing sustainable revenue for the projects we publish on. Our aim at Packt is to establish publishing royalties as an essential part of the service and support a business model that sustains Open Source.

If you're working with an Open Source project that you would like us to publish on, and subsequently pay royalties to, please get in touch with us.

Writing for Packt

We welcome all inquiries from people who are interested in authoring. Book proposals should be sent to author@packtpub.com. If your book idea is still at an early stage and you would like to discuss it first before writing a formal book proposal, contact us; one of our commissioning editors will get in touch with you.

We're not just looking for published authors; if you have strong technical skills but no writing experience, our experienced editors can help you develop a writing career, or simply get some additional reward for your expertise.

About Packt Publishing

Packt, pronounced 'packed', published its first book "Mastering phpMyAdmin for Effective MySQL Management" in April 2004 and subsequently continued to specialize in publishing highly focused books on specific technologies and solutions.

Our books and publications share the experiences of your fellow IT professionals in adapting and customizing today's systems, applications, and frameworks. Our solution-based books give you the knowledge and power to customize the software and technologies you're using to get the job done. Packt books are more specific and less general than the IT books you have seen in the past. Our unique business model allows us to bring you more focused information, giving you more of what you need to know, and less of what you don't.

Packt is a modern, yet unique publishing company, which focuses on producing quality, cutting-edge books for communities of developers, administrators, and newbies alike. For more information, please visit our website: www.PacktPub.com.

Zenoss Core Network and System Monitoring

ISBN: 978-1-847194-28-2   Paperback: 280 pages

A step-by-step guide to configuring, using, and adapting this free Open Source network monitoring system - with a Foreword by Mark R. Hinkle, VP of Community Zenoss Inc.

1. Discover, manage, and monitor IT resources

2. Build custom event processing and alerting rules

3. Configure Zenoss Core via an easy to use web interface

4. Drag and drop dashboard portlets with Google Maps integration

OpenVPN

ISBN: 978-1-904811-85-5   Paperback: 272 pages

Learn how to build secure VPNs using this powerful Open Source application

1. Learn how to install, configure, and create tunnels with OpenVPN on Linux, Windows, and MacOSX

2. Use OpenVPN with DHCP, routers, firewall, and HTTP proxy servers

3. Advanced management of security certificates

Please check **www.PacktPub.com** for information on our titles

Learning Nagios 3.0

ISBN: 978-1-847195-18-0   Paperback: 316 pages

A comprehensive configuration guide to monitor and maintain your network and systems

1. Secure and monitor your network system with open-source Nagios version 3

2. Set up, configure, and manage the latest version of Nagios

3. In-depth coverage for both beginners and advanced users

Learning FreeNAS

ISBN: 978-1-847194-68-8   Paperback: 244 pages

Configure and manage a network attached storage solution

1. Turn a PC into a Network Attached Storage server with FreeNAS

2. Configure, manage, and troubleshoot your FreeNAS installation

3. Up to date with the latest FreeNAS release

4. Includes a comprehensive troubleshooting section

Please check **www.PacktPub.com** for information on our titles

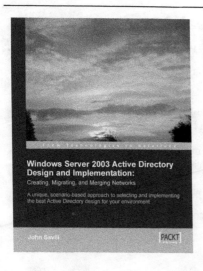